SHEM FLEENOR

*Marketing the Magic City:*

*Miami and the Making of Modern America, 1896 - 1920s*

**1848 Publishing Company**

New York and Melbourne

ISBN-13: 978-1-951231-00-2

## Table of Contents

**Introduction** ................................................................. 3

**Chapter One** ................................................................ 23

"Nature and Anxiety in Mass Marketing of Miami"

**Chapter Two** ................................................................ 34

"Nationalism and Anxiety in Mass Marketing of Miami"

**Chapter Three** ............................................................. 62

"White Supremacy and Anxiety in Mass Marketing of Miami"

**Chapter Four** ............................................................... 78

"Masculine Supremacy and Anxiety in Mass Marketing of Miami"

**Chapter Five** ............................................................... 117

"Capitalism and Class Anxiety in Mass Marketing of Miami"

**Coda** ........................................................................ 140

## Introduction

Modernity and consumerism can both be incredibly abstract and difficult to define. *Marketing the Magic City: Miami and the Making of Modern America, 1896 - 1920s*, as such, begins by qualifying and defining related, if not conflated, definitions of modernity and consumerism. This is intended to help the reader better navigate the mass marketing of South Florida from the 1890s through the 1920s analyzed in the pages that follow.

Oxford University Press's *Patterns of World History* elaborates that the most dramatic effect of World War I was that the single pattern of modernity associated with the nineteenth century – constitutional and ethnic-linguistic nationalism and scientific-industrial society – splintered into three competing subpattens early in the twentieth century. These three subpatterns were capitalism-democracy, socialism-communism, and supremacist nationalism. The United States was, according to Oxford, the nation most associated with capitalism-democracy. Fascist Germany, Italy, and Japan were associated with supremacist nationalism.[1] The Soviet Union was most closely associated with socialism-communism. These "three modernities," according to Oxford, competed through World War II. After the supremacist nationalism championed by Adolf Hitler, Benito Mussolini, and Tojo Hideki was widely discredited, the Cold War confrontation between American and Soviet modernity fell into sharp

---

[1] Peter von Sivers, Charles Desnoyers, and George Stow, *Patterns of World History*, (New York, Oxford University Press, 2015) 855.

relief, and ultimately fueled the Cold War. Both superpowers scrambled to establish political partnerships and economic ties with so-called non-aligned post-colonizing countries. After the fall of the Berlin Wall in 1989, American consumer capitalism and democracy became, according to Francis Fukayama, the hegemonic form of modernity, supposedly signaling the end of the ideological battle between capitalism and communism that had fueled history through the twentieth century.[2]

Oxford's three subpatterns of modernity form the framework through which the mass marketing of Miami, as elaborated in the pages that follow, is examined. Miami, however, sometimes supports and defies Oxford's definition of modernity. Despite Oxford's useful tripartite definition, marketing of Miami illuminates that defining modernity can be incredibly paradoxical.

Associating modernity with mass consumption, however, helps to somewhat demystify both concepts. Martin Daunton and Mathew Hilton, for example, define consumption as a broad economic, social, and cultural process. Mass consumption has sometimes been erroneously deemed a less central and

---

[2] See Fukayama's *The Last Man and The End of History*, (New York, Free Press, 1992). Fukayama argues that a remarkable consensus concerning the legitimacy of liberal democracy as a system of government had emerged throughout the world, as it conquered rival ideologies like hereditary monarchy, fascism, and most recently communism. He argues that liberal democracy may constitute the end point of mankind's ideological evolution and the "end of history." Despite Fukayama's optimism, the end of the twentieth century and beginning of the twenty-first century witnessed the emergence of new and unanticipated challenges to the domination of the capitalist-democratic order. For instance, Russia and China's transition from communism to capitalism illuminates that autocracy is as compatible with capitalism as it was with communism.

less serious institutional sphere of inquiry than production — a view related, to some degree, to denigrating consumption as "women's work."[3] Consumerism is, however, very important and by no means frivolous because it illuminates a profound economic, social, and cultural shift from thrift to profligacy in "average" Americans' values in the early decades of the twentieth century. Mass consumption is also a hallmark of American modernity, which is in stark contrast to the austere deprivation associated with the Soviet-style modernity. The affluent leisure imbued in marketing of Miami, in fact, often unwittingly depicted modern America as the antithesis of Soviet-style modernity, which was most often Taylorist in its depictions of Soviet modernization and transformation from agricultural to industrial.

Though Miami's image was often depicted as the anecdote and antithesis of Soviet style modernity, the "Magic City" likewise helps to illuminate that supremacist nationalism and capitalism were not quite, as Oxford deduced, competing forms of modernity; they, in fact, fueled each other in the decades before and after World War I. Miami's image thus illuminates "modern" race relations in which white supremacy was as central to the urbanization of the New South, including Miami, as it was to the Old South's rural plantocracy. And though marketing of Miami in the early decades of the twentieth century at times

---

[3] For more on gendering of production and consumption in American cities, see Mark Gottdiener, *The Theming of America: Dreams, Visions and Commercial Spaces* (Boulder, CO: Westview Press, 1997). See also Richard Butsch's edited volume, *For Fun and Profit: The Transformation of Leisure into Consumption* (Philadelphia: Temple University Press, 1990).

seemed to celebrate the dawn of the "New Woman," it simultaneously celebrated Victorian gender norms, especially heteronormative family values. And while Miami was being marketed as an epicenter of social mobility, the get-rich-quick ethos associated with the "Magic City" ultimately ended in countless calamites for nearly all but the most affluent real estate barons. In short, beneath the air of leisure and liberation imbued in Miami's commoditized form, the celebration of consumer capitalism embedded in the "Magic City's" image was profoundly conformist and conservative and ultimately served the interests of the existing social order. In that sense, the American brand of modernity rooted in mass consumption is, perhaps above all else, best understood as a marketing construct shilling old wine in "new and improved" bottles, adding to the Marxist adage that one of the primary mechanisms that make the endless accumulation of capital possible is the commodification of everything, including nationalism, race, gender, and class.

In addition to affluent leisure, Miami's commoditized form was also, as the chapters that follow illuminate, heavily imbued with nationalism, racial and gender supremacy, and mixed with utopian promises of social mobility. The cultural shift from thrift to profligacy in American society associated with the rise of urbanization and mass consumption in the late-nineteenth and early twentieth century helps to illuminate that the more pervasively American economic development was fueled by consumerism, the more prominently class, perceived gender differences, and racial mores were reified in the marketing of Miami.

The utopian abundance celebrated in Miami's commoditized form, however, belies the incredibly flawed American democracy in the Jim Crow South. Nearly thirty percent of Miami's residents by the start of the 1920s were black people who were deprived the franchise and full citizenship in New South Miami. Most American women were likewise prohibited from voting in the first two decades of Miami's existence. American women, however, won the right to vote, in part due to their importance to the American economy, during World War I. The "Great War" also pushed millions of African-Americans out of the South to industrialized cities north of the Mason-Dixon Line, which nationalized the republic's festering racial problem at a time when millions of immigrants were also flooding into American cities. Most advertisements for Miami were intended for a national audience – for consumers who had never been to South Florida before. Ads portrayed Miami as a haven for white men and illuminated a great deal about the racial gendering of mass consumption and the modernization of America. The most prominent way real estate barons and boosters assuaged anxiety towards American modernity and attracted white consumers to frontier South Florida was by imbuing "value" in the region via culturally charged advertisements that promised "proper" racial and gender mores and overtures of social mobility.

*Marketing the Magic City* is a cultural history that examines advertisements of South Florida in the early decades of the twentieth century. Miami, which has always been a product as much as an actual place, was sometimes simultaneously depicted as a natural oasis, southern yet Eurocentric, as a white man's utopia, and as a bastion of consumer capitalism.

The advertisements all have utopianism in common. Utopian ads for Miami were ultimately designed to seduce consumers and investors to South Florida by any means necessary. All these "utopian" depictions of Miami as a harbor for anxious white men collectively betray a great deal of American anxiety related to industrialization and urbanization that manifested itself in an adoration for a mythic nature that seemed to be increasingly imperiled, but also manifested itself in racism, sexism, nationalism, and belief that consumerism, especially in a supposedly utopian resort city such as Miami, was a panacea for class conflict. But these ads were not merely helping to make Miami. Miami, and the ads that made it, were also remaking America into an urban and industrial nation concomitant to gradually making Americans into a people who first considered their personal and national identities in the realm of consumerism, rather than the work they did or class, race, or ethnicities to which they belonged.

Gunther Barth and Eugen Weber argue that print commodities can be powerfully transformative. They cite the turn of the twentieth century's new agencies of culture, particularly the metropolitan press, department stores, stadia, and vaudeville houses, which, they argue had important educative functions that helped to mold the lives of provincials throughout the Atlantic World from rural folk into "city people." Peter Fritzsche, who studies turn-of-the-twentieth-century Berlin, likewise argues for reciprocity between cities and the ubiquitous print media spawned, in part, by urbanization between the "built city" and the "word city" that provided a social text for the reading of urban space as a geographical, cultural, social, and political site. The "word city," Fritzsche argues, performed a number of crucial tasks. At a basic level, print commodities interpreted the city, stabilized its fluidities, typologized its citizens, and mapped its expanding terrain. Print commodities, in short, helped to make the city "usable" for the growing ranks of consumers arriving there from the hinterland by advertising housing and jobs, and by cataloging the diversions and pleasures of the city for a mass readership avid to enjoy the promise of higher wages and increased leisure time.

John Henry Hepp likewise regards a city's print commodities as important material artifacts that shed light on the broader cultural impulses of the time. The discourse of the popular press, including promotional materials, Barbara Berglund argues, is exactly what connects the embodied practices of the urban everyday with imperial nation-making. Berglund evokes Marshall McLuhan's belief that print helped to produce the nation state. Print, especially moving images, moved society from an oral culture to a literate culture, but also introduced a capitalist society in which there was clearer class distinction and more pronounced and celebrated sense of individualism in the context of the consumer market, even though Americans gradually thought less in terms of the class they belonged to than the products and services they consumed.

Print commodities that marketed Miami, in short, were not merely selling consumers the "Magic City," they were also crafting urbane consumers/modern Americans. The centrality and importance of mass marketing as it regards Miami's industrial development and urbanization cannot be overemphasized, especially considering the frontier-turned-resort city was so vital to attracting vacationers and homeseekers (which also lured scores of workers from across the American South and the Caribbean) to South Florida in the early decades of the twentieth century.[4] The primary sources especially essential to the book that follows are thus promotional brochures, maps, newspapers, and postcards, but also newsreels, music, movies, and sundry other ephemera produced by local commercial-civic elites who were often in league with northern investors. The

---

[4] For more on the workers drawn to Miami in the early decades of the twentieth century see Raymond A. Mohl, "Black Immigrants: Bahamians in Early Twentieth-Century Miami." *The Florida Historical Quarterly*, Vol. 65, No. 3 (Jan., 1987), pp. 271-297; see also Melanie Shell-Weiss, "Coming North to the South: Migration, Labor and City- Building in Twentieth-Century Miami," *The Florida Historical Quarterly*, Vol. 84, No. 1, Special H-Florida Issue: Florida History from Transnational Perspectives (Summer, 2005), pp. 79-99; and Shell-Weiss's *Coming to Miami: A Social History* (Gainesville, Fla: University Press of Florida, 2009); and also Robert Cassanello and Melanie Shell Weiss, eds. *Florida's Working-Class Past: Current Perspectives on Labor, Race, and Gender from Spanish Florida to the New Immigration* (Gainesville, Fla. University of Florida Press, 2009).

utopian primary sources analyzed in the pages that follow span the 1890s – 1920s. They collectively amount to early Miami's commodified form. They also provide readers with a tapestry of how Miami might have appeared to consumers who had never before been to South Florida.

The ads depicting South Florida as utopian seem to have worked quite well. By the 1920s, thanks in part to often hyperbolic reports, songs, postcards, billboards, brochures, and a barrage of ads in national magazines and newspapers, subdivisions were sprouting all across southeast Florida, with the most prime parcels of land nestled on secluded and exclusive barrier islands.[5] Despite the questionable wisdom of building a subtropical city wedged between the Atlantic Ocean and a vast alligator, mosquito, and viper-infested swamp, Miami's population more than doubled in the first decade of the twentieth century. In 1910 alone, consumers from more than ninety cities, twenty-five states, and three foreign countries spent cash in South Florida.[6] As a result of a gain in population of 440 percent, "The Wonder City of America" also grew faster than any other in the U.S. from 1900 to 1920.[7] It was estimated that more

---

[5] *Directory of Newspapers and Periodicals,* Philadelphia 1952; see also Jeanne Bellamy, "Newspapers of America's Last Frontier," *Tequesta,* No. XII, 1952.

[6] Larry R. Youngs, "The Sporting Set Winters in Florida: Fertile Ground for the Leisure Revolution, 1870–1930," *The Florida Historical Quarterly,* Vol. 84, No. 1, Special H-Florida Issue: Florida History from Transnational Perspectives (summer, 2005), pp. 57–78.

[7] "Miami by-the-Sea," (Miami Chamber of Commerce), 1922. Smathers Special Collections, Ephemera Collection, University of Florida; see also, U.S. Bureau of the Census, *Fourteenth Census of the United States,* 1920, Population, III (Washington, 1922), 197. From 1910 to

than 300,000 visitors also vacationed in Miami every twelve months.[8] During the first half of the 1920s, Miami's population almost doubled in the winter season, which lasted from November to early April. And by 1925 Miami outranked every other city in the U.S. in per capita housing construction.[9] By the end of that year *The Miami Herald* had set a world record with 42,500,000 lines of advertising, mostly for South Florida real estate and tourist attractions.[10] In the 1920s alone, Miami's total population increased by a staggering 100,000 residents, many of whom were lured to South Florida by advertisements, including stories made to seem as though they were news, that depicted the region as a utopia site of easy social mobility where traditional racial and gender hierarchies reigned supreme.[11] This astonishing growth prompted pundits such as T.H. Weigall, a British advertising agent who visited Miami in 1925, to report, "It was impossible

---

1920, Miami's population increased by 440 percent, totaling 29,571. Until 1920, not a single city with a population of more than 50,000 had developed in South Florida. Miami was the seat of Dade County, which led all Florida counties with a 258-percent growth rate.

[8] "Miami by-the-Sea," (Miami Chamber of Commerce, Miami, Fla., 1924), Smathers Special Collections, Ephemera Collection, University of Florida.

[9] "Some Miami and Dade County Statistics," *The Miamian* 5 (February 1925), 14.

[10] Kenneth Ballinger, *Miami Millions: The Dance of the Dollars in the Great Florida Land Boom of 1925*. (Miami, FL: Printed by The Franklin, 1936. Print). See also Jeanne Bellamy, "Newspapers of America's Last Frontier," *Tequesta*, No. XII, 1952.

[11] James Carney, "Population Growth in Miami and Dade County, Florida," *Tequesta*, No. 6, 1948.

to open a newspaper anywhere in the United States without finding some reference to Florida and Florida's activities."[12]

Consumer technologies, especially ads perpetuated in newspapers, newsreels, records and cinema, worked synergistically to create the notion of "value" in the South Florida frontier, which helped to fuel Miami's tourism and real estate industries, ultimately luring blue-collar workers from places such as the American South and the Bahamas, as well as well-to-do white consumers from across the United States, all through the early decades of the twentieth century. The demand created by residents and tourists for homes, hotels, and sundry goods and services meant opportunity for many folks who wanted to live in South Florida as builders, clerks, mechanics, small business owners, and gentry. An ever-expanding manual labor force in building construction, stevedoring, road building, hotels and railroad work also stoked the rapid growth of Miami in the early decades of the twentieth century.[13] As such, by the height of the South Florida real estate boom in 1926, products such as leisurewear, auto parts, mattresses, baked goods, paints, drugs, hats, and perfume were made in Miami.[14]

---

[12] T. H. Weigall, *Boom in Paradise* (New York, 1932), 136.

[13] C.S. Thompson, "The Growth of Colored Miami," *The Crisis* 4:83–84, 194.

[14] Frank B. Sessa, "Miami on the Eve of the Boom: 1925," *Tequesta,* No. XI, 1951.

Despite Miami's lack of vital infrastructure (such as state-of-the-art sanitation and water filtration systems) and the city's remoteness from the northeastern megapolis (never mind no air conditioning), by 1916 the value of annual building permits in Miami was an impressive $2,000,000.[15] But hospitality accommodations were often inadequate and unable to meet demand, which cost the city's business owners untold profits. Miami's image as a consumerist utopia as hailed in an array of state-of-the-art mass media channels, in short, superseded its reality as a resort city in many regards early in the city's existence. In 1917, for instance, hotels turned away an estimated 10,000 vacationers anxious to indulge in the sun, fun, excitement, and luxury that had, in large part due to advertising, become synonymous with the "Magic City;" ads of which seduced more consumers to Miami each winter season, many of whom decided to stay year-round.[16]

Utopian advertising, to reiterate, was a key catalyst in Miami's astounding growth and development in the early decades of the twentieth century. The chapters that follow thus focus on specific motifs in ads of South Florida to analyze the text for wider cultural meaning and importance in terms of the

---

[15] *Miami Herald*, December 31, 1916.

[16] *Fourteenth Census of the United States,* 1920, Volume I and II, Population (Washington, D.C., 1922), 195; *Fifteenth Census of the United States*, 1930, Volume I, Population (Washington, D.C., 1931), 23; see also Thomas A. Castillo, "Miami's Hidden Labor History," *The Florida Historical Quarterly*, Vol. 82, No. 4 (Spring, 2004), pp. 438–467; 442.

United States' rapid evolution into the world's premier commercial empire. Chapter one is titled "Nature and Anxiety in Mass Marketing of Miami." It elaborates the conspicuous conflation of Miami as a natural utopia in order to tease out national anxiety associated with urbanization and industrialization. Miami's urbanization and industrialization were fueled, quite ironically and somewhat comically, by its image as a suburban middleway between the rural agrarianism associated with the Deep South and the rapid urbanization of the northeast U.S. and Western Europe in the early decades of the twentieth century.

Miami was thus a harbinger of the suburban modernity that so heavily shaped the American experience in the decades after World War II. Chapter two is titled "Nationalism and Anxiety in Mass Marketing of Miami." The ads in chapter two especially betray national anxiety associated with new immigration in the early decades of the twentieth century, a time in which the nature of American identity seemed to be changing drastically, which created a great deal of anxiety, particularly in the hearts and minds of white supremacist Nativists. Chapter three is titled "White Supremacy and Anxiety in Mass Marketing of Miami." It is chocked full of ads that associate Miami with white supremacy, which collectively helped to establish Miami as a white man's domain in the hearts and minds of American consumers, both black and white. Chapter four, "Masculine Supremacy and Anxiety in Mass Marketing of Miami," much like the ads in chapter three, thoroughly depict Miami to be a heterosexual white man's fantasy, teeming with unattended bachelorettes. The ads in chapter four particularly depict women to be objectified as sexual objects. It is vital to note that these depictions, which were surely, at least in part, a reaction to the vibrant suffragette movement that transpired concomitant to the publication of many of these ads, elaborate a great deal about masculine anxiety to increased economic and political mobility of American women. They also help to elucidate that the ascendance of American consumer culture was largely fueled by the sexual objectification of white women at a moment in history when women were demanding basic human rights, such as the right to have formal political identities of their own. Chapter five is entitled, "Capitalism and Anxiety in Mass Marketing of Miami." Notions that real estate in Miami promised workers social mobility effectively exploited workers' anxiety towards new immigrants, women, African Americans, and automation displacing them. The ads in chapter five also prominently depict South Florida to be a site of quick and easy social mobility, and, therefore, likewise underscore the relationship between the rise of mass marketing in tandem with casino capitalism in the decades since the Gilded Age.

The pictures above demonstrate the rapid transformation of Miami from frontier into city and emerging market. Lincoln Road, March 1905; Lincoln Road construction site (Miami Beach, Fla.), Hoit Collection, Pancoast and Collins family papers, 1901-1982, Series 3: Photographic prints and certificates, 1905-1955, Historical Association of South Florida (top). Lincoln Road, 1935, South Florida photograph collection, 1870-2011, Series 1, Drawer 1, Folder 364, Historical Association of South Florida (bottom).

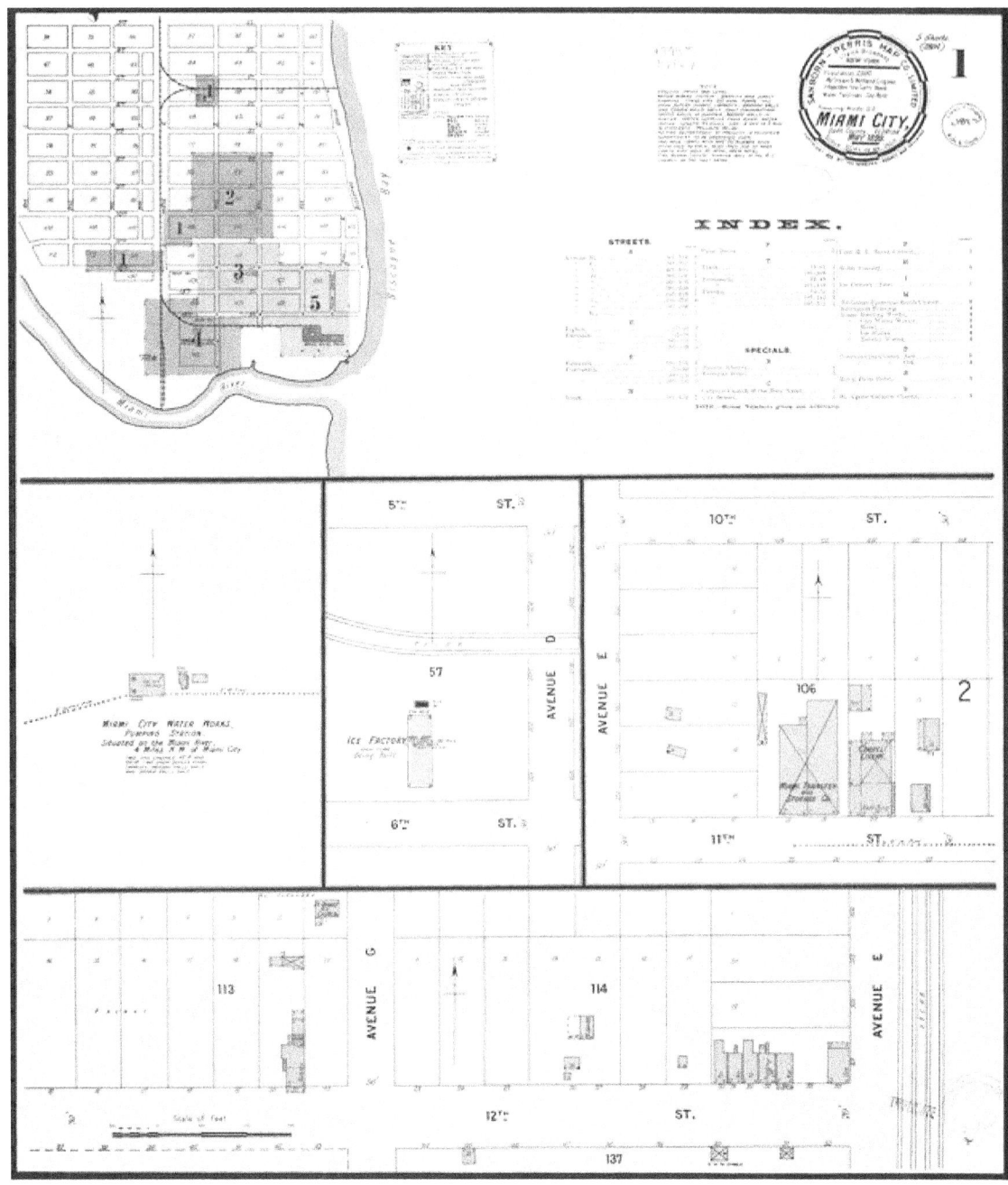

This 1899 Sanborn Fire Insurance map demonstrates how desolate Miami was after only three years of existence. The concentration of property (and property values) is based on proximity of the structures to Henry Flagler's Royal Palm Hotel in the southeast section of the city wedged between two Florida East Coast Railway Lines. "Colored Town," the antipodal of Flagler's properties, is in the northwest section of the city. "Colored Town's" "value" was, according to Sandborn Insurance assessors, scant compared to Flagler's lands. These maps are particularly instructive because they give a kind of tangibility to "value" associated with real estate in Miami as it was first evolving into a city. They also demonstrate how racism was woven into South Florida's real estate markets.1899 Sanborn Fire Insurance Map, P.K. Yonge Florida Maps Collections, Sanborn Map Company, New York, George A Smathers Library, University of Florida.

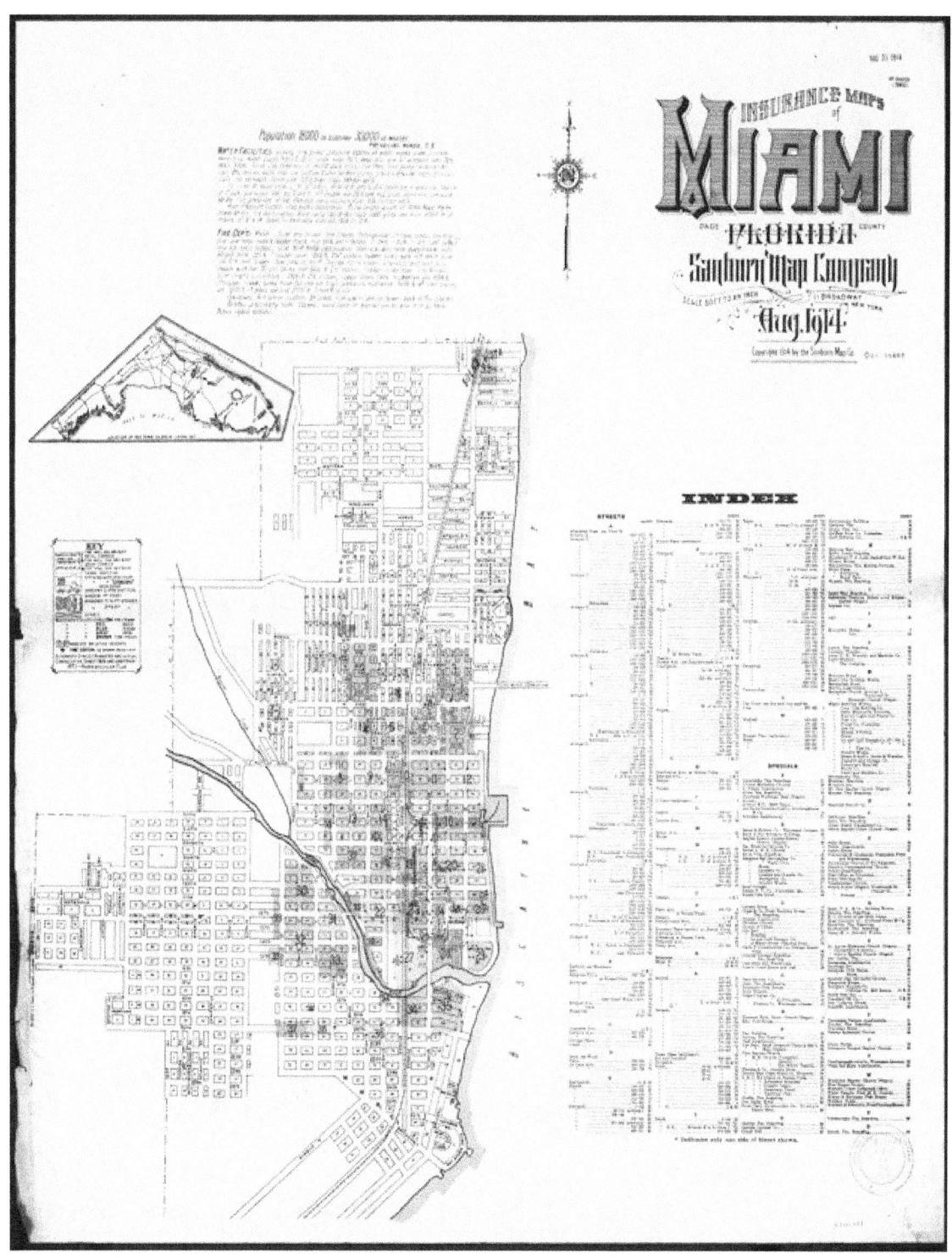

By World War I, Miami was fast developing into one of the nation's premier resort cities. Notice how the city's geographic domain is also rapidly expanding from one Sandborn map to the next. The value of property reflects the city's growing importance to American consumers and investors. 1914 Sanborn Fire Insurance Map, P.K. Yonge Florida Maps Collections, Sanborn Map Company, New York, George A Smathers Library, University of Florida.

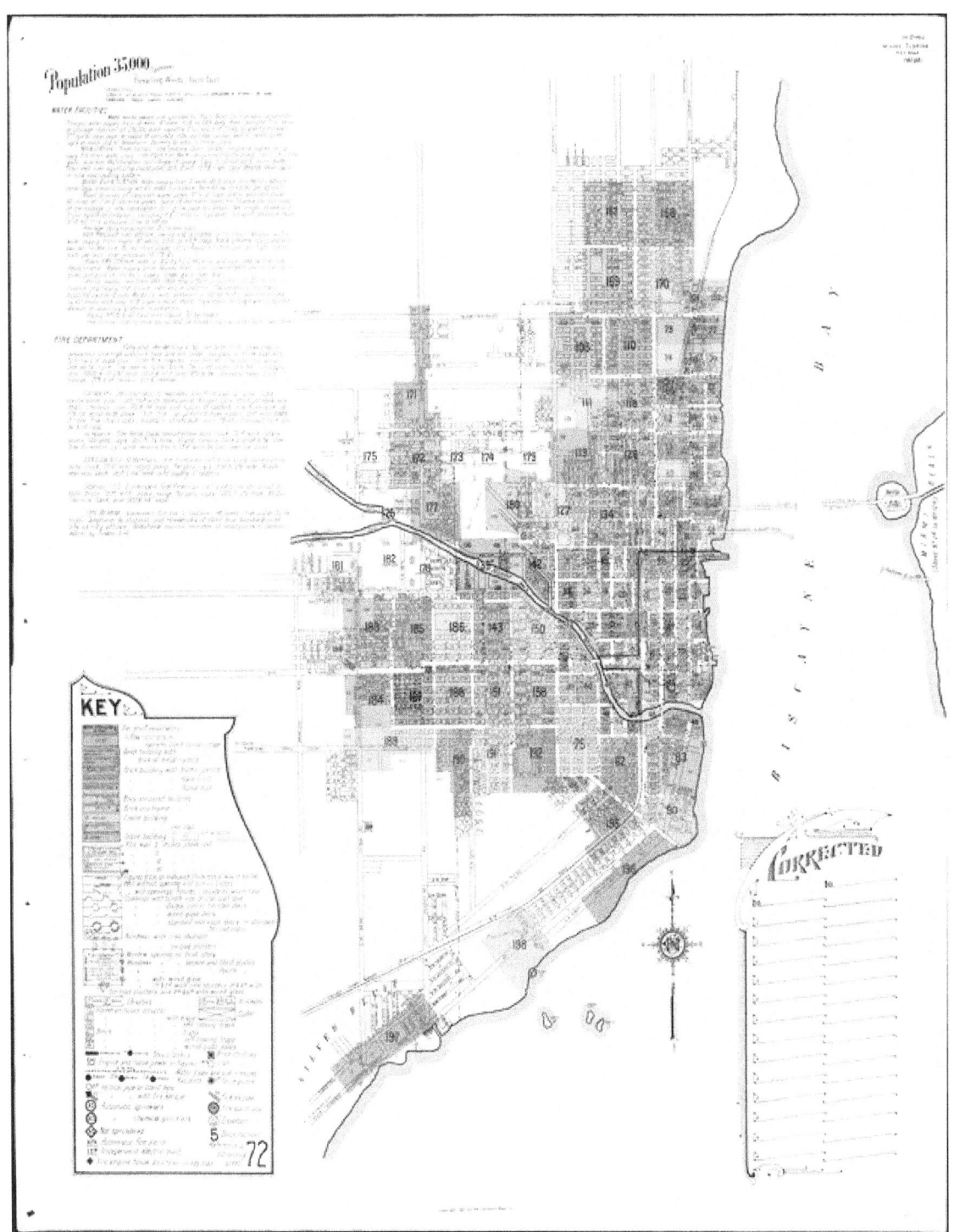

By 1924, the South Florida real estate "boom" had nearly peaked and Miami's geographic size, population, and property values and population were growing steadily along with its geographic boundaries. But again, notice the northwest section of the city and how patchwork and undeveloped the area surrounding "Colored Town" is to the rest of the city. 1924 Sanborn Fire Insurance Map, P.K. Yonge Florida Maps Collections, Sanborn Map Company, New York, George A Smathers Library, University of Florida.

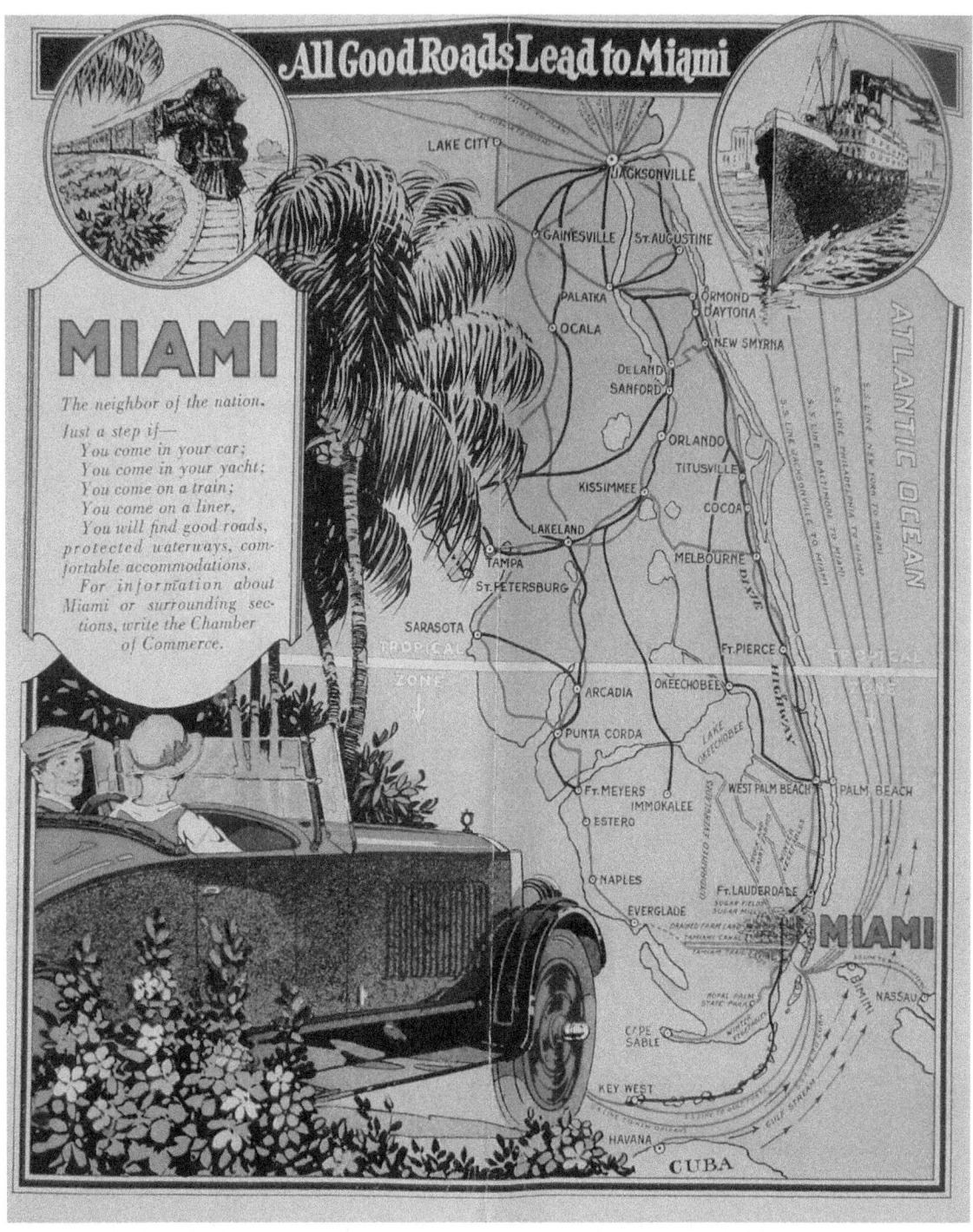

Note the text at upper left, which reads: "Miami: The Neighbor of the Nation. You come in your car; You come in your yacht; You come on a train; You come on a liner; You will find good roads, protected waterways, comfortable accommodations..." Cuba is included in the picture, demonstrating the synergy between roads, rail, steamship, consumerism, and the ever-expanding reach of the U.S.'s commercial empire in the decades before World War II. "All Roads Lead to Miami," travel brochure, Miami Beach Chamber of Commerce, Early 1920s, 3; Smathers Library Ephemera Collection, University of Florida, Gainesville; Folder 37, number 1066.

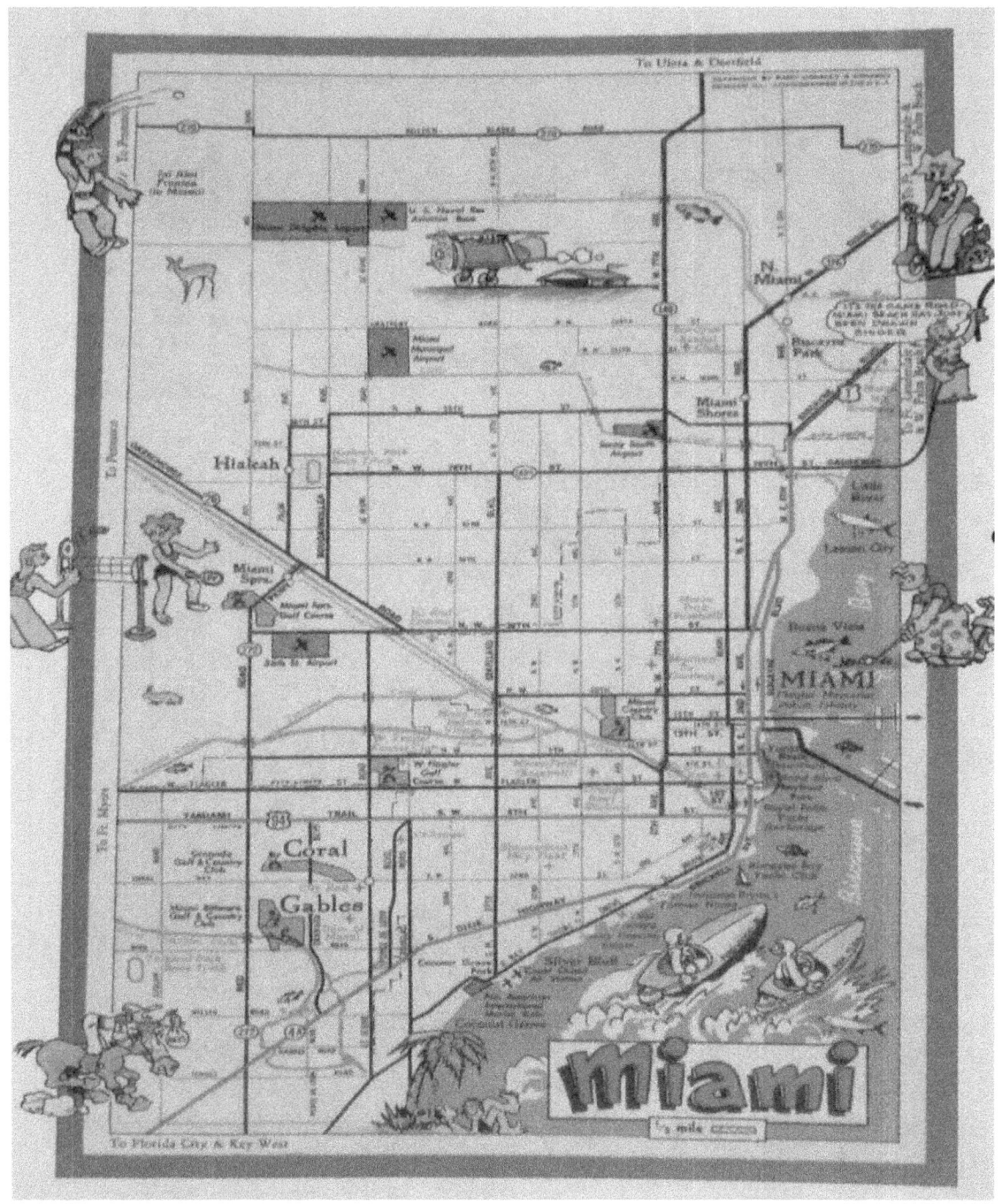

Note the miles of roads and highways stretching in all directions, ample leisure opportunities, and sun, fun, and nature imbued in Miami's commoditized form. These depictions made Miami and modern America seem like the antithesis of Soviet-style modernity. Note also that all the consumers depicted in the image are white and engaged in idle luxury. It is also interesting to note that "Colored Town" and "Lemon City," where Miami's black residents were concentrated, are not depicted on the map at all. "A Vision of American Modernity," Gulf Oil Map (and advertisement) of/for 1920s Miami. *Patterns of World History* (New York, Oxford University Press, 2016), 864.

# Chapter One

## "Nature and Anxiety in Mass Marketing of Miami"

E.P. Thompson viewed religion as a weapon used by employers to discipline the working classes,[17] but in Miami during the early decades of the twentieth century, mass consumption was sometimes conflated with the supernatural.[18] For instance, Sunday school picnics featuring William Jennings Bryan helped to attract thousands of Southern Baptists to the "Magic City." Bryan's *Bible*-thumping oratorical powers could reportedly "paint a word picture that had buyers seeking lots in great stampedes." He was so unrepentantly effusive in his descriptions of South Florida that he boasted that Miami was "the only city in the world" where a person could "tell a lie at breakfast" that would "come true by evening." He attributed Miami's supernatural qualities and real estate values not to boosterism or seductive advertising, but rather to the fact that Miami had a superabundance of "what the people must have… God's sunshine."[19] South Florida was, in short, often depicted to be, by the likes of Bryan and myriad ads, as a supernatural site of social transcendence.

---

[17] E. P. Thompson, *The Making of the English Working Class* (London, Pelican, 1963).

[18] For more on traditional Christianity accommodating consumer culture, see William Leach, *Land of Desire: Merchants, Power, and the Rise of a New American Culture* (New York: Pantheon Books, 1993).

[19] *Miami Herald,* January 16, 1925.

Prior to Miami's incorporation in 1896, the area around Biscayne Bay was a tiny village adjacent to Fort Dallas, which was built by the federal government during the Second Seminole War in 1836, and was used primarily as a supply station and refuge. A half-century later, the frontier was largely unchanged by human hands. In 1882, for example, a newspaper editor described South Florida as "a region mysterious, unknown, beautiful — a terra incognita — of which as little is known as the center of the Dark Continent (Africa)." In 1889, adventurer James Davidson published his "Guide for Florida Tourists and Settlers," in which he likewise described South Florida as a place where "there can be nothing but insects, vermin, mud, malaria, Indians, desolation, abomination, discomfort, disease, black death, and poverty where nothing will grow but comptie and mangroves, and where nobody lives."[20] A year later, the United States census recorded fewer than 400,000 people in all of Florida and no more than 2,400 on the peninsula south of Lake Okeechobee. In 1892, a tourist guide described Dade County as a "wild and uninhabitable district, in the main inaccessible to the ordinary tourist, and unopened to the average settler."[21] As late as 1894, when the Florida East Coast Railway first steamed into West Palm Beach, 70-miles north of what would later become Miami, Fort Dallas served

---

[20] See Christopher E Meindl, "On the Eve of Destruction: People and Florida's Everglades from the late 1800s to 1908," *Tequesta*, Number LXIII, 2003.

[21] James Davidson, "Guide for Florida Tourists and Settlers," (Norton, 1892), 19.

primarily as a trading post for Seminole Indians and the Brickell family, who lived on the south bank of the Miami River.[22]

But from 1896 through the 1920s Miami was seemingly miraculously carved from wilderness and integrated into the modern American commercial empire and economy through massive public works projects, such as the making of the Port of Miami, and the manufacturing of real estate markets around railways, canals, and roads leading in and out of South Florida. The development of travel technology together with communication technology such as the ads examined in this study synergistically facilitated the transformation of Miami from frontier to a tourism and real estate Mecca, which ultimately laid the foundation for a new urban and consumerist order in South Florida's soil and identity, which was sometimes depicted in ads to be preternatural, which helped to codify Miami as the "Magic City."

Miami's growth, development, and very existence were products of the Gilded Age/Progressive Era — a time when cities were increasingly constructed around notions of profits and social progress. But the Progressive Era is also somewhat paradoxically associated with an admiration for nature, which seemed to be vanishing as a result of the rapacious nature of Gilded Age capitalism, most

---

[22] The Brickell's, a patrician family settled in the Biscayne Bay area in 1871 after leaving Cleveland, Ohio. The family traded wares with Seminole Indians who paddled up the Miami River from their homes in the Everglades. The Brickell's owned land adjacent to Julia Tuttle's property; See *Miami Herald*, January 18, 1980; and also see Frederick P. Wilson, *Miami, From Frontier to Metropolis* (Miami, 1956), pp. 14 – 16.

notably the exploitation associated with industrialization and urbanization. The Progressive Era helped foster the establishment of the National Park System (1916), which was designed to protect the wilderness from the rampant exploitation of nature associated with the Gilded Age. Marketers of Miami ironically cashed in on the preservation craze deeply associated with anxiety towards industrialization to urbanize South Florida.

Commercial entrepreneurs throughout the New South, including South Florida, during the Progressive Era, much like the industrialists in William Cronon's *Nature's Metropolis: Chicago and the Great Midwest,* often saw the world in terms of markets, commodities, profit margins, investments, debts, and efficiency. As such, a natural resource particularly vital and valuable in South Florida was millions of square miles of undeveloped property, lots of which lay in swampland. Real estate developers all throughout South Florida — most notably Henry Flagler — quietly acquired options on huge expanses of land surrounding their prospective ventures, incorporated land and development companies, sold stock to raise money to purchase optioned land, advertised their burgeoning enterprises, and staked out imaginary streets, carving land into potential profits. Ads conspicuously depicting South Florida as a natural oasis ripe for exploitation were ultimately meant to imbue value in the region's burgeoning real estate industry, which was made possible by travel technology (such as Flagler's Florida East Coast Railway) and communication technology (such as the primary sources examined in this study).

The Progressive Era, which rail and real estate baron Henry Flagler and northern industrialists precipitated, and of which Populists such as William Jennings Bryan and also Florida Governor Napoleon Bonaparte Broward (1905 – 1909) were products, was partly defined by notions that society could be holistically transformed to, like a corporation, work as efficiently as possible. The *Pensacola Journal*, for instance, supported government intervention in reclamation of the Everglades because "tens of millions of acres of the most fertile lands imaginable" would be transformed "from dismal and pestilential swamps and useless bogs" into highly prosperous homes, to become the "garden spots of the nation."[23] Populists such as Broward, who hoped to attract disgruntled northern factory workers to farms in Florida, likewise believed that taming the Everglades for yeoman could potentially offset the travails commonly associated with urbanization and industrialization. There were even popular tunes written in the interest of exploiting South Florida swamps with choruses such as "Down in the Everglades, I've got a little love for you," that helped transform the idea of South Florida from frontier wasteland into "black gold" and respite from the social

---

[23] Edward T. Layton Jr., *Revolt of the Engineers: Social Responsibility and the American Engineering Profession* (Cleveland, 1971), 1–10; and also Aaron D. Purcell, "Plumb Lines, Politics, and Projections: The Florida Everglades and the Wright Report Controversy," *The Florida Historical Quarterly*, Vol. 80, No. 2 (Fall, 2001), pp. 161–197; and also *Pensacola Journal*, April 1, 1906, 10.

despair and degradation commonly associated with northern cities during the Progressive Era.[24]

What was originally seen to be a detriment – the fact that Miami was a frontier and very difficult to get to by land and sea – was often commonly depicted by early advertisers of South Florida as what actually made the region such an attractive destination compared to soul stealing factory work and tenement housing commonly associated with cities such as New York City, Chicago, Cleveland, and Boston.

The mass marketing of Miami through the 1920s, in fact, betrays American anxiety in regard to the vanishing of nature and changing of the nation's collective identity from rural and agrarian to urban and consumerist as a result of rapid industrialization and immigration. It is therefore not as ironic as it might initially seem that Miami's urbanization was, in part, the result of its image as a natural utopia and anecdote to and antithesis of northern urbanization.

Ads such as those depicting Miami as a natural wonder and oasis from the perceived social despair and degradation associated with life in urban-industrial centers throughout the Atlantic World paid quick dividends. By October of 1911 – just fifteen years after Miami's incorporation – *The Metropolis,* Miami's most popular newspaper at the time, reported that Miami's suburbs, which were

---

[24] Isador Cohen, *Historical Sketches and Sidelights of Miami* (Miami, Fla., 1925), 85.

wedged against the Everglades and Atlantic Ocean, were booming with new construction.[25] And the more ads depicted South Florida as virgin nature aching for exploitation, the more people actually arrived. And the more people arrived, the more value South Florida real estate markets actually had.

Image, in short, helped define the reality of Miami's urbanization. And by-and-by, despite how underdeveloped, remote, and dangerous frontier South Florida remained into the second decade of the twentieth century, Miami was, in fact, emerging into something akin to the real estate market and world-renowned resort city venture capitalists such as Henry Flagler had only dared to dream of a generation earlier.

---

[25] *Miami Daily Metropolis*, October 11, 12, 1911.

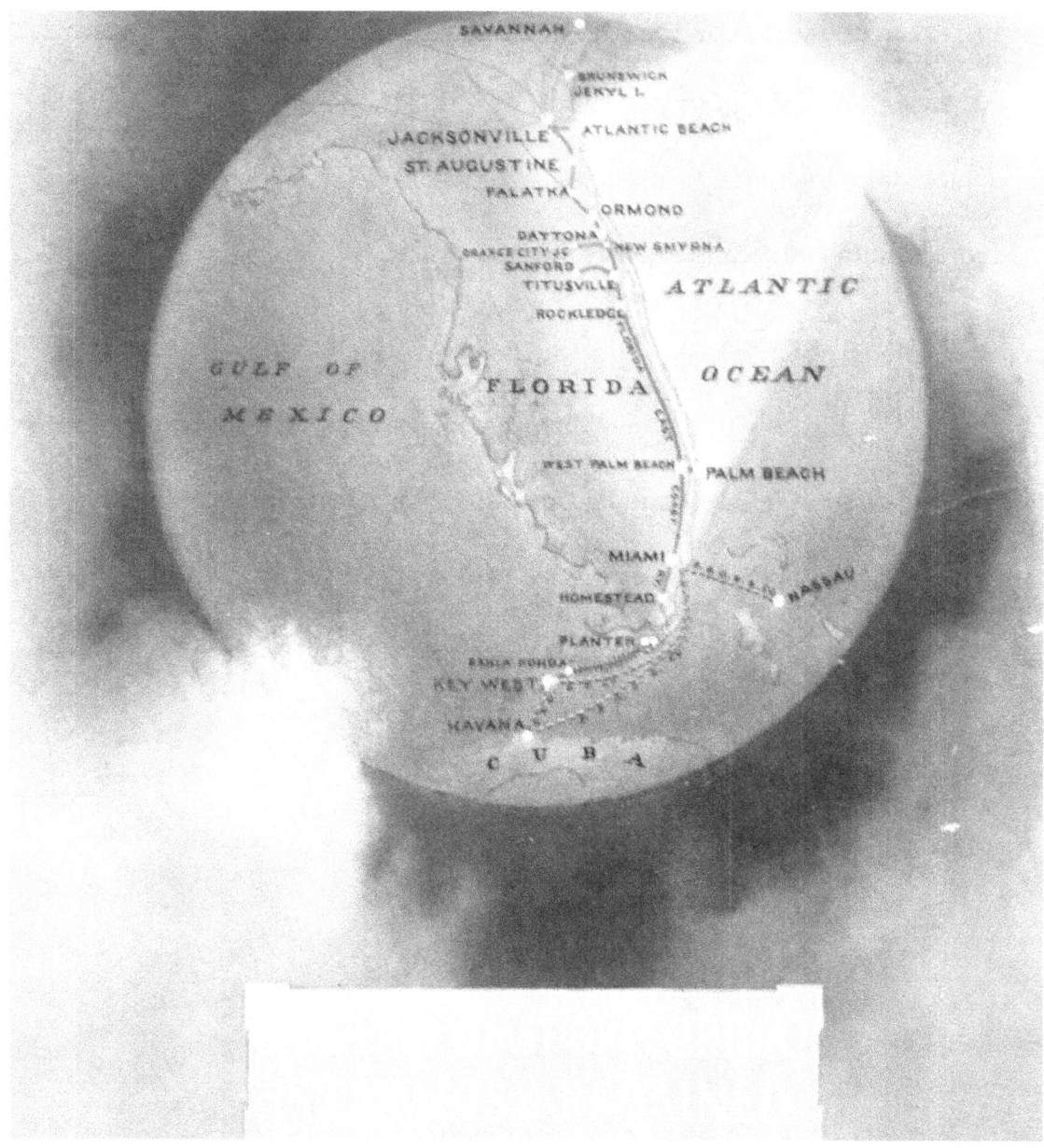

This brochure which advertises hotels along Florida's east coast has a caption at the bottom center of the page that reads, "The East Coast of Florida is Paradise Regained," which especially demonstrates that Florida was being defined as a preternatural place in mass marketing. Note how a kind of divine light is bringing the east coast of Florida, much of which was frontier at the turn of the twentieth century, into the light of capitalism. The notion of "paradise regained," which was often used to market Florida's east coast in the early decades of the twentieth century, speaks to the notion of paradise lost associated with urbanization of cities such as New York, Chicago, and Cleveland. Also note how Cuba, Miami, and other southern cities are made into a transnational tourism market linking the New South with the Caribbean at the very moment the U.S. was emerging as a global commercial empire. Florida East Coast Railway and Hotels, 1902, Florida Historical Society Archive, Cocoa, Florida, PAM Collection, box 12, folder 4.

Note the locomotive piercing the frontier at center surrounded by luxury hotels (property values). Also note the synergy between the commodification of nature, agriculture, and vacationing with the train, which is a symbol of urbanization, industrialization, and modernity. "Florida East Coast Railway and Hotels," 1902, Florida Historical Society Archive, Cocoa, Florida, PAM Collection, box 12, folder 6.

Modern mass marketing and pop culture, including songs such as this, helped to rebrand the Everglades from pestilential wilderness to "black gold" waiting to be exploited by intrepid yeoman. "Down in the Everglade," Van Alstyne Egbert, 1906, New York City, Duke University Special Collections, Sheet Music Collection, 1900 – 1909.

Note the iconic News Tower (at top right of the postcard) and the smoke stacks of factories (at top left). This postcard is particularly instructive because it depicts Miami as a natural wonder yet also industrialized. The image, in fact, speaks to the centrality of mythology to early marketing of Miami, considering Miami had no smoke stacks to match South Florida's superabundance of nature. Miami's urban-industrial development was fostered by consumerism rather than the kind of industrial production associated with smoking chimneys of factories in places like New York, Boston, Cleveland, and Chicago. "The Causeway connecting Miami and Miami Beach, Florida" postcard (J.N. Chamberlain and Fairchild Aerial Camera Corporation, Miami Beach Fla., 1926); aerial view of the causeway looking west, Historical Association of South Florida, Stan Cooper Collection, 1870 to 1938; series 4, subseries 1: postcards, box 1, folder: "Miami Beach."

# Chapter Two

## "Nationalism and Anxiety in Mass Marketing of Miami"

Three days before Christmas in 1886, at Delmonico's restaurant in lower Manhattan, *Atlanta Constitution* editor Henry Grady regaled the New England Society of New York, including financier J.P. Morgan, and Standard Oil's Henry Flagler, who within a decade would become known as "the Father of Miami."[26] The New South "is enamored of her new work," Grady lauded. "Her soul is stirred with the breath of a new life. The light of a grander day is falling fair on her face. She is thrilling with the consciousness of growing power and prosperity."[27] Grady basked a moment in a warm wave of optimistic applause. But his syrupy romanticism of the South as a region completely redeemed was —

---

[26] William Tecumseh Sherman, who Grady joked was "a careless man about fire," a not-so-subtle jab at the general for torching the orator's beloved hometown, Atlanta, Georgia, to ash during the Civil War a quarter-century earlier, was also in attendance.

[27] Grady's New South speech to the New England Society of New York, December 22, 1886. The "New South" broadly includes themes elaborated in C. Vann Woodward's *Origins of the New South, 1877–1913* (Louisiana State University Press, 1951). General themes in *Origins* include the striving of a new class to drag an agricultural society into the industrial age, the struggle of impoverished farmers to create a new political culture, the rise of racial segregation, and the triumph of progressivism for whites only. Woodward only slightly addresses the relationship to southern urbanization, tourism, and the rise of mass consumption in the U.S. For more on "progressivism for whites only," see Arthur S. Link, "The Progressive Movement in the South, 1870–1914," *North Carolina Historical Review*, 23 (1946), 172–73.

at best — as much fantasy as factual.[28] Grady's dream for the New South, however, in some ways became reality in Miami from 1896 through the 1920s.[29]

The city's first newspaper, Flagler's *Miami Metropolis*, had particularly taken on a duty beyond that of publishing the usual local, national, and world news. *The Metropolis*, which opened for business May 15, 1896 (more than two months before Miami was even incorporated), sought to sell ad space concomitant to attracting new settlers and developers to the Gold Coast by depicting the "Magic City" as a virgin and tropical paradise ripe for commercial exploitation and settlement. The paper also consistently and conspicuously defined Miami as southern.[30] The first issue of the paper, for example, boasted that readers were fortunate enough to hold the most "southern newspaper" on the U.S. mainland, published at the "most southern railroad point in Uncle Sam's domain," and at the "most southern" telegraph terminal and express office on

---

[28] Grady, and also Richard Edmonds, the editor of the *Manufacturers' Record*, often inflated southern possibilities and morphed them into southern achievements via print commodities. New South boosterism often blurred into fraud, especially when referring to "enlightened" race relations in the New South. But Grady's boosterism also represents the sense of utopianism that starkly contradicted harsh postbellum realities New South boosters sought to obscure and/or transcend in the late-nineteenth and early twentieth century.

[29] Miami did not, like Grady's Atlanta, "rise phoenix-like" from the ashes of the Civil War. Grady's vision of a "New South," according to William Link, represents an attempt to forget and transcend the Civil War as much as to develop the region's economy; see Link's *Atlanta, Cradle of the New South: Race and Remembering in the Civil War's Aftermath* (Chapel Hill: University of North Carolina Press, 2013).

[30] Print commodities shilling Miami were not merely fueling industrial synergy; they were themselves increasingly profit-generating industries, especially in first-generation Miami, where, by 1930, newspapers garnered $4,250,000, profits annually. F. Page Wilson, "Miami: From Frontier to Metropolis: An Appraisal," *Tequesta*, No. 15, 1955, 39.

the mainland at "Marvelous Miami."[31] The urban ethos perpetuated in products such as *The Metropolis,* together with sundry pamphlets and brochures produced by real estate barons and municipal governments, defined the city as a commercial enterprise above all else, which was often sold to southerners and northerners alike as a New South city.[32]

Ads (including those published in local newspapers such as *The Metropolis* and national newspapers such as *The New York Times* and magazines such as *McClure's* and *The Saturday Evening Post*), together with transportation networks such as railroads and automobile highways (such as the Dixie Highway), helped to insinuate Miami as well as northern cities into the mythic "Cult of the Confederacy" that was so popular in the United States in the decades before and after D.W. Griffith's *Birth of a Nation* (1915) premiered. New and/or improved transportation systems and communication technologies (such as more sophisticated and utopian mass marketing), together with the nation's railroads and new highways also helped to codify Miami as a New South city, even though it had no Old South history.

---

[31] *Miami Metropolis,* May 15, 1896.

[32] For comparison: ice manufacture was $2,090,000; cement products $1,515,000; and ice cream manufacture, $1,275,000; See Millicent Todd Bingham, "Miami: A Study in Urban Geography," *Tequesta,* No. 8, 1948.

Miami — unlike Birmingham, Atlanta, Nashville, and the Carolina Piedmont — was wedged between a vast swamp and the Atlantic Ocean. As such, Miami could not sustain large manufacturing or refining operations like Atlanta and Birmingham could. The marshlands surrounding Miami also did not harbor many minerals worth refining. The swampy Everglades outside Miami seemed to promise no value in a capitalist market other than the potential fertility of the soil, lots of which the state of Florida and private industrialists alike foolhardily hoped to drain with a series of canals extending from Lake Okeechobee to the Atlantic Ocean and Gulf of Mexico.[33] Attempts to turn the Everglades on the outskirts of Miami into the nation's sugar bowl and state's breadbasket, however, proved exceedingly difficult and unprofitable.[34] Thus, from an economic viability standpoint, first-generation Miami faced a glaring and dystopian crisis of legitimacy from the moment the city was incorporated.[35] Miami has, as such, always been an especially image and publicity conscious

---

[33] The number of manufacturing plants in Greater Miami by 1930 was 210 (see U.S. Census 1930). The smallest company employed only a few workers; other companies employed several hundred workers. In order of capital invested, these industries were rated as follows: newspapers, $4,250,000; ice manufacture, $2,090,000; cement products, $1,515,000; and ice cream manufacture, $1,275,000. In other words, mass consumption was synergistic to many other industries in Miami. See Bingham, "Miami: A Study in Urban Geography," *Tequesta*, No. 8, 1948.

[34] William A, Graham. "The Pennsuco Sugar Experiment," *Tequesta*, No. XI, 1951.

[35] Miami, due to its lack of natural resources, was plagued by a "crisis of legitimacy," which could be overcome only through the immense power of stylish mass media deeply imbued with gender, race, class, and nationalism. Roland Marchand found that in the early twentieth century, large corporations faced a "crisis of legitimacy" rooted in consumers' inability to keep pace with production; see his, *Creating the Corporate Soul: The Rise of Public Relations and Corporate Imagery in American Big Business* (Berkeley: University of California Press, 1998), 3.

city. Due to its geography and dire economic outlook, it had to be. It had to sell — not automobiles or other ready-made products, per se — but itself: its homes, leisure, luxury, sun, fun, excitement, promise of social mobility, sex, yet conservative racial and gender norms, and especially its utopian image.[36] Its image, in short, made Miami seem like a viable commodity even before the frontier had become a budding real estate market and city. Miami's image as a southern yet Eurocentric city, in short, imbued value in frontier South Florida.

The most prominent connection between Miami and Nashville's urbanization was the industrial production of popular culture. Whereas Nashville became home to the incredibly popular Grand Ole Opry (opened in 1925), which simultaneously celebrated tradition and modernity (defined here as urbanization and the industrialization of mass consumption). But what particularly links Miami to other New South cities is similar iconography in mass marketing. Miami, which did not exist during the American Civil War, was conspicuously marketed as the "Jewel of the South" and "'Magic City' of the Southland."

The marketing-fueled urbanization of the New South, particularly frontier South Florida, ironically and paradoxically depended on the very forces — a

---

[36] "Information was needed and columns poured from city hall, Frank Sessa wrote, "mostly, however, about glamorous events and bathing beauties to catch more datelines;" See Frank Sessa, "Miami on the Eve of the Boom: 1925," *Tequesta,* No. XI, 1951.

national consumer market, transportation infrastructure, a strong federal government, and mass marketing — that threatened the traditional agrarian and southern "state's rights" vision of American identity and constitutionalism. And by the time of Miami's rise, rapid urbanization north of the Mason-Dixon Line, which was largely characterized by millions of new Immigrants from Southern and Eastern Europe as well as black migrants from the American South and Caribbean, consumer culture had helped to reify the notion that the South, which now included Miami, was more American and yet simultaneously cosmopolitan and exotic than northern industrial centers such as New York and Chicago. And as the uniformity and alienation of the industrialized order supposedly threatened to destroy western civilization, Americans found that they could find a balm for their anxieties in southern spas and resort towns such as Miami, which were increasingly marketed in national newspapers, magazines, and sundry other ephemera as havens for white consumers seeking respite from the social despair and degradation often associated with the urban-industrial dynamo north of the Mason-Dixon line.

Myriad brochures were mailed to homeowners throughout the country, and housewives were often the first to consume them during the day in the midst of tending to chores and children. The marketing paid dividends. By 1925 — the height of the South Florida real estate boom — two million Yankees vacationed in Dixie. Many of them also purchased parcels of property and became full-time residents of South Florida.[37]

Miami's image as a southern city deep in the heart of Dixie was carefully calculated to attract white tourists from both the South's hinterlands as well as Nativists from northern cities. And when asked why promotional brochures produced by the Miami Chamber of Commerce were target-marketed to tourists rather than homeseekers, City Commissioner E.G. Sewell answered, "once here, they'll sell themselves the homes."[38] He was prescient. From 1915 to 1925 – the decade concurrent with his tenure as head of the Miami City Commission – boosterism, advertising, and mass marketing symbiotically helped to exponentially increase building investment and tourism in Miami.[39]

The depiction of Miami as a southern city coincided with the early decades of the twentieth century, a time when the United States was rapidly evolving into a global empire fueled by white supremacy, which was concomitant to scores of black Americans increasingly fleeing the lynch terror and second-class citizenship associated with the Deep South for industrialized

---

[37] William A. Link review of Dewey W. Grantham, *The South in Modern America: A Region at Odds*, in *Southern Cultures*, Volume 3, Number 1, 1997, pp. 83–87.

[38] Sewell, a Georgian by birth, was one of the "Magic City's" marketing masterminds. Soon after the formation of the Miami Chamber of Commerce in 1913, Sewell became chairman of its publicity department. Sewell was, according to historian Paul George, "a public relations genius with a flair for the dramatic." See George, "Passage to the New Eden: Tourism in Miami from Flagler through Everest G. Sewell," *The Florida Historical Quarterly*, Vol. 59, No. 4 (April, 1981), pp. 440-463; 449.

[39] The rampant real estate speculation between 1921 and 1926 in Miami not coincidentally coincided with five years of city-manager government, many of whom, like Sewell, were deeply invested in speculative ventures along the Gold Coast.

northern cities. The marketing-fueled urbanization of Miami as a southern city also coincided with a time in American history when a nationalized nostalgia and fetish for the antebellum era, as evidenced by the wild popularity of *Birth of a Nation*, was increasingly common throughout both the North and the South. Miami's image was, accordingly and somewhat ironically, depicted as a southern city, despite the fact that the city's suburbanization was made possible by the economic intervention and largesse of Henry Flagler, a northern rail and real estate tycoon who might have otherwise been viewed as a carpetbagging personification and symbol of the industrialized Union's defeat of the Confederacy, which was fighting for the agrarian slavocracy that had for so long shaped southern politics and identity in contrast to the rest of the nation.

Miami also had an especially high proportion of black migrants from the Bahamas and the American South's hinterlands (nearly thirty percent by 1920), which particularly made the articulation of South Florida as a white man's utopia in accordance with Old South cultural values and social mores especially prevalent amongst boosters like Sewell, a Georgian, who was likely anxious to obscure the necessity and centrality of black labor to Miami's rise as a world-renowned resort city.

The advertising that helped to underwrite Miami's rise in the early decades of the twentieth century also helped to cultivate an image of Modern America as white supremacist, southern, yet global at a moment in history when the United States had recently defeated the Spanish Empire in both the eastern and western hemisphere, transforming the former backwater of Europe from a continental to global commercial empire stretching all the way from the Philippines to frontier South Florida. Advertisements for early Miami thus depicted the city as southern, American, and global.

By the 1920s, ads for South Florida regaled consumers with fantastical ideas such as, "Castles in Spain are now available."[40] The ad marketed a neighborhood in George Merrick's "master suburb," Coral Gables, which was thousands of miles and an ocean away from Spain. British ad-man T.H. Weigall likewise referred to Miami as "an incredible tropical paradise with immense, brilliantly lit castles towering among the stars and voluptuously-attired semi-Eastern, semi-Italian ladies and gallants drifting in the foreground in spacious gondolas."[41] In 1925, *The New York Times* also described Miami with a headline that read "Not a Mushroom Town: Rich In Tropical Fruits, the Vicinity is Growing Into an American Riviera."[42] On April 15, 1925, near the zenith of the South Florida speculative frenzy, Addison Mizner's development corporation conflated the New South with Europe when it announced that Boca Raton, which

---

[40] Phillip E. DeBerard, Jr., "Promoting Florida: Some Aspects of the Uses of Advertising and Publicity in the Development of the Sunshine State" (Unpublished M.A. thesis, University of Florida, 1951), 65–66.

[41] T. H. Weigall, *Boom in Paradise* (New York: Alfred H. King, 1932), 18.

[42] *The New York Times*, "Millions of Capital Drawn to Miami," March 15, 1925, section two, 1.

is just north of Miami, was the "social capital of the south" and the "Venice of the Atlantic."[43]

Miami, which is just ninety miles from Cuba, was often depicted to be a Eurocentric city deep in the heart of Dixie. This seemingly duplicitous marketing of Miami helped to rapidly transform South Florida's image from a remote and largely uninhabitable dystopian frontier that was indomitable to even the Union Army, into a cosmopolitan American resort city in an ever-expanding global empire rooted in the increased purchasing power (thanks in part to credit/debt) of the nation's working classes.

The U.S.'s ascendance all through the twentieth century into a position of global dominance coincided with, and was inseparable from, the dominance of an American-style consumer culture ("soft power") and economy over international spaces, but also national places such as frontier South Florida, whose value was concocted in part by the celebration of the antebellum South, which obscured the cruel reality of Jim Crow in housing and labor markets.

The rise of the American Empire at the end of the nineteenth century and early decades of the twentieth century, in short, did not just happen in places like Cuba, Puerto Rico, Guam, and the Philippines; it also happened in frontiers

---

[43] *Palm Beach Post*, April 15, September 1, 1925, February 26, July 14, 1926; *Boca Raton: Florida's Wholly New Entirely Beautiful World Resort*, MDC Files; Donald W. Curl, "Boca Raton and the Florida Land Boom of the 1920s," *Tequesta*, No. XLVI, 1986, pp. 138–45.

turned suburban resort cities such as first-generation Miami, which, when one considers Jim Crow, was a a colonial enterprise. Miami's commoditized southern/global/American identity ultimately helped to map an idealized American history, tradition, mythology, and ideology across the continent (including frontier South Florida) and beyond by defining an organic white nationalism that linked American identity to a shared landscape and mythology mass marketed as history. Marketing of Miami thus involved not just selling the city, but also selling white supremacy as American consumer culture, and class and empire packaged as the new nationalism, which was, as the chapters that follow illuminate, thoroughly racialized and gendered.

This 1915 brochure particularly demonstrates the conflation of Miami as a "Magic City" in the New South. Note the iconography, particularly the juxtaposition of nature, white women, leisure, and modern travel technology. "The Magic City of the South Land: The Land of Sunshine and Flowers," (J.N. Chamberlain, 1915), University of Florida Special Collections, Ephemera Collection, Smathers Library, Folder 38, number 1101.

Ads for Miami substituted swaying palm trees for the magnolias popular in ads for other New South cities like Tampa, Nashville, and Atlanta. "Miami, Jewel of the South," (J.N. Chamberlain, Miami, Fla., 1920), University of Florida Special Collections, Smathers Library, Ephemera collection, Folder 44, number 1240.

This image juxtaposes slaves picking cotton on a plantation with white sunbathers at the beach. In other words, the plantation system was being codified as part and parcel of white leisure and used to market tourism and mass consumption in Miami and many other cities in both the North and South, which illuminates how popular the "Cult of the Confederacy" was as The U.S. rapidly industrialized into a global empire. "Dixie Route to Florida," (Poole Brothers Printing, Chicago, mid-1920s); Smathers Ephemera Collection, University of Florida, folder 26, number 2574.

Note the "Old South" iconography, including a Civil War battle, and Victorian gender norms — including men in midst of duel, as well as a "happy helper" onlooker. Ads such as the one above for the "the scenic route through Dixie," of which Miami was the most southern destination, is particularly peculiar considering the city was founded in 1896 and thus had no Civil War history. "Dixie Route to Florida," (Poole Brothers Printing, Chicago, mid-1920s); Smathers Ephemera Collection, University of Florida, folder 26, number 2574.

This 1903 drawing in a brochure advertising South Florida refers to the Gold Coast of Florida as the "American Riviera." This item is particularly interesting not only because of the allusion to Europe, but also because the frolicking women don Victorian garb, as opposed to the heavy emphasis on the Flapper/New Woman motif common in marketing of Miami during the 1920s. "A Comedy of the American Riviera," Florida East Coast Hotel Co., 1900 – 1909. University of Miami Library, Special Collections, ASC9999, PS3500.A1 C55 1903.

Many Europeans and Americans were particularly interested in Native Americans, who seemed to be going extinct at the turn of the century. This 1910 brochure marketing the Florida East Coast Railway and properties, including hotels and parcels of land in South Florida, exhibits a white woman dressed as an Indian atop an aristocratic coat of arms. Aristocracy and the "Noble Savage" were both in high fashion amongst European and also American industrialists such as Henry Flagler, who owned the hotels marketed in this brochure, and the train that would escort consumers to Florida's mostly frontier Atlantic coastline. "Florida East Coast: List of Hotels and General Information Concerning the Famous Winter Resort Section of America," Florida East Coast Railway, Saint Augustine, Fla., page 1. University of Miami Library Special Collections. ASC9999 F309. F54. 1910/11.

Note the architectural similarity of Henry Flagler's Royal Palm Hotel to Versailles. Miami was conspicuously crafted to be the best of the Old World mixed with the best of the New World, thereby blurring the distinction between ancient and modern. "Royal Palm Hotel, east front," (Pictorial Centre, 1910s, Miami). Postcard collection, folder: Miami hotels, Florida State Archives, Tallahassee, Florida.

Note how this image at once alludes to the moonlight and magnolia iconography associated with New South cities, but also simultaneously alludes to Italian/Mediterranean, and high culture iconography. Miami could at once be depicted as nostalgic for the antebellum era and also simultaneously a global (suburban) city. "Miami Beach, Florida," (St. Augustine, Florida Record Co., 1923); University of Miami Special Collections, image number ASC9999, F319.M62M48 1923.

This 1925 brochure marketing Coral Gables depicts the suburb as "Miami Riviera," with "40 miles of water front" property. The insinuation of Miami as both a city in the American South and Atlantic World speaks to how global the world's real estate market was becoming in the early decades of the twentieth century as the U.S. evolved into the world's premier commercial empire. "Coral Gables, Miami Riviera: 40 Miles of Waterfront," Coral Gables Corporation, 1925. University of Miami Library, Special Collections, ASC9999 F319. C8 C674.

This image depicts Seminole Indians gazing from afar at a Venetian gondola parked in front of a Mediterranean-style waterfront mansion. The text in this ad alludes to Miami as a modern consumerist utopia. "Miami By the Sea, The Land of Palms and Sunshine," Miami Chamber of Commerce, 1926, page 4. University of Miami Library, Special Collections, ASC9999 F319.M6 M6227 1926.

The outside of the brochure above evokes historical fictions in vibrant colors such as the utopian fountain of youth. Here, Miami is marketed to retirees, and it promises an easier and extended life, as well as implicitly available young women. Also note the juxtaposition of idyll beach scene, coupled with Spaniards (presumably conquistadors) chasing Indians (presumably Calusa), as Miami's marketers tried to cash in on the historical tourism craze popular throughout the Imperial Atlantic in the decades after the U.S. defeated the Spanish Empire in a war that helped to transform the U.S. into the world's premier commercial empire. "Miami: Golden Sunshine Adds Golden Years," (Hollywood Press, Miami, Fla. 1927); Smathers Library Special Collections, Ephemera Collection, University of Florida. Folder 39, number 1121.

The conspicuous blending of Miami's identity with the Spanish Empire (particularly conquering conquistadors), as seen above, especially evokes the conflation of Miami with utopianism and national prominence. A generation earlier, the U.S. had become a global empire after it defeated Spain in the Spanish-American War (1898) and pushed the not-yet-industrialized European empire out of the western hemisphere. This ad is inside a brochure designed presumably to lure retirees with beach scenes, the promise of an easier and extended life, and young contortionists and other implicitly available collections of young women. The outside of the brochure evokes historical fictions in bright colors such as Ponce de Leon's quest for the Fountain of Youth. The text cashes in on the utopian notion that spending winters in Miami can "add ten years to your life." "Miami: Golden Sunshine Adds Golden Years," (Hollywood Press, Miami, Fla. 1927); Smathers Library Special Collections, Ephemera Collection, University of Florida. Folder 39, number 1121.

Though Miami was often marketed as a cosmopolitan and exotic world city and/or New South city, it was also very common to see images in which an American flag was prominently displayed at the shoreline. The centrality of American flags to marketing of Miami helped to brand frontier South Florida as an American bastion of capitalism. Marketers of Miami often conspicuously depicted South Florida as an American domain readymade for white consumers. The use of the American flag in marketing of Miami also helped rebrand South Florida from a desolate frontier into one of the world's wealthiest cities by the end of the twentieth century. "The Lure of the Southland: Miami and Miami Beach, Florida," (C.H. Ward, Miami, Fla., 1915), Smathers Special Collections, Ephemera collection, University of Florida, Folder 42, number 1179.

The opening of the Dixie Highway with the southernmost terminus of the highway in Miami helped solidify South Florida's status as both quintessentially southern but also an international city. The Romanesque victory arch that greeted motorists to Miami also alludes to the neoclassical architectural fetishism associated with the Roman Empire that was popular in American history since the nation's inception. "Miami, Jewel of the South," (J.N. Chamberlain, Miami, Fla., 1920), University of Florida Special Collections, Smathers Library, Ephemera collection, Folder 44, number 1240.

Note the American flags flapping atop the victory arch, which at once alludes to the Roman Empire and American Civil War. The victory arch also connects Miami with Montreal, which underscores how global America's consumer market was becoming in the early decades of the twentieth century. "The Lure of the Southland: Miami and Miami Beach, Florida," (C.H. Ward, Miami, Fla., 1915). Smathers Special Collections, Ephemera Collection, University of Florida, folder 42, number 1179.

This image helps imbue the notion of wealth, grandeur and ultimately "value" in Miami. Note also the American standard waiving high above the hotel, making Miami into a consumerist utopia, symbol, and frontier outpost of the burgeoning global commercial empire. "Hotel Halcyon, built of Miami stone - Miami, Florida," (Chaille and son, Miami, late-1910s), postcard collection, folder: Miami, Florida State Archives, Tallahassee, Florida.

Industrialist James Deering's palatial Vizcaya, a Mediterranean-style mansion surrounded by gardens comparable to Versailles's, like Flagler's Royal Palm Hotel, helped imbue value into South Florida's real estate industry by depicting the region as European. "Ground of Vizcaya, the James Deering Estate," E.C. Kropp, 1920s, University of Miami Special Collections, Coral Gables, Florida Postcard collection, series, 2, box 3, folder: "Miami."

Even when marketers of Miami sought to establish the city as a growing metropolis, nature and eurocentrism was a central aspect of ads. This postcard does a particularly good job illuminating how Miami was a concocted spectacle as much as city. Here, the city's skyline is depicted as an impressionistic (nineteenth century French movement) painting juxtaposing skyscrapers with sailboats. Impressionism was, in part, a commodification of nostalgia for a nature that seemed to be disappearing due to industrialism and urbanization. Miami was, conversely, depicted to be a suburban oasis. "Skyscraper hotels on Miami's waterfront - Miami, Florida," (Gulf Stream Card & Distribution Co., 1920s, Miami), postcard collection, folder: Miami, Florida State Archives, Tallahassee, Florida.

# Chapter Three

## "White Supremacy and Anxiety in Mass Marketing of Miami"

Urban space particularly mediates the relationships that define national, urban, and personal identities.[44] Public space also serves as an important arena for struggles over public power, resources, and values. Groups, in short, secure broad recognition of their identities by colonizing public spaces, especially in cities.

Such was the case in Miami from the 1890s through the 1920s, as evidenced by postcards depicting the Ku Klux Klan as masters of urban spaces in contrast to racial "others" as rural, pre-modern, and politically impotent (see below). Promotional brochures, postcards, and sundry other ephemera promoting Miami thus depict an urban consumerist society with whites who are synonymous with power firmly in control of urban spaces and by implication the consumer market, in stark contrast to racial "others" who are far removed from urban spaces and also removed from consumerism, which is synonymous with American modernity.

In the decade after the premiere of D.W. Griffith's *Birth of a Nation* (1915), Klan membership boomed in South Florida. And by 1925, the local Klan chapter had an estimated 1,500 members, a large sum considering Miami was home to

---

[44] Eric Avila, *Popular Culture in the Age of White Flight: Fear and Fantasy in Suburban Los Angeles* (Berkeley: University of California Press, 2004), xiv.

just 70,000 citizens, 30 percent of whom were black.[45] In 1923, The John B. Gordon Number 24 order paraded from Flagler Street along North Bay Shore Drive to the county causeway to Palm Island. Thousands lined the parade route, and hundreds watched as a cross burned to ash.[46] Symbolizing their "crusade against ignorance and miscegenation," the Klan's float featured three hooded knights with swords drawn next to a dragon with "The Enemies of American Ideals" blazoned on it. "American ideals," according to the float, seemed to be synonymous with white supremacy and racial segregation. The dragon, for instance, appears primed to protect a kindly white child outside a red schoolhouse. The float, not surprisingly, won first prize.[47] This type of public spectacle played itself out in New South cities all across the region in the early decades of the twentieth century. Few New South boosters were, however, as publicity conscious as marketers of Miami, some of which conspicuously used postcards of the Klan to market Miami to the world beyond Biscayne Bay.

This spectacle in early 1920s Miami, like so many other racist spectacles (such as lynching) throughout the urban Atlantic World during the Jim Crow/Apartheid era, was ultimately designed to project the notion that the

---

[45] *Daily Metropolis*, May 24, 25, 1921; *Miami Daily News*, July 26, 1925; *Miami Herald*, November 24, 1925.

[46] It was estimated that 2,500 automobiles were parked along the causeway; see Frank B. Sessa, "Miami on the Eve of the Boom: 1925," *Tequesta*, No. XI, 1951.

[47] *Washington National Kourier*, January 1, 1924.

"Invisible Empire" was prepared to employ political violence to protect and defend white supremacy of urban spaces. But as much as the Klan's use of spectacle was calculated to establish Miami as a white man's haven, reports of such vigilantism also helped to racially codify South Florida for a national audience of consumers. In addition to segregated housing and job markets, consumer advertising such as the postcards below, which were designed to seduce consumers to Miami by any means necessary, circulated anti-black stereotypes across the nation and propagated the cultural association between white consumers and black objects/servants as synonymous with the "Magic City's" brand.

White Supremacy, as the postcards above and below indicate, was a defining feature of southern urbanization. Segregation, as it took full legal form in the 1880s and 1890s, was a response to urbanization and deliberately deprived urban blacks of dignity and equality. The alliance between working-class and bourgeois white northerners and southerners as the New South industrialized and urbanized reflected a widespread conviction that disfranchisement, segregation, and voter proscription was not only the foundation of a supposedly rational social system of racial control, but that it also promised a greater measure of social stability, economic development, and white political unity.

Since Miami was so nascent, groups such as the KKK, as well as city fathers, many of whom were real estate barons, sought to establish the city as a white man's haven in contrast to northern cities, which were increasingly peopled by foreigners and black Americans in the early decades of the twentieth century, especially after World War I. The symbolic racial violence propagated in newspapers, ads, and political discourse was symbiotic to political violence in Miami. The industrialization of second-class citizenship, which was as rooted in racially segregated housing and labor markets as it is with disenfranchisement, was reified by racist ads of Jim Crow Miami that depicted both black Floridians and Seminole Indians as subservient, sometimes imperiled, but always politically impotent rural caricatures in contrast to urbane and sophisticated white consumers and leisure seekers as is depicted in chapter five of this study.

Miami, an enterprise almost totally dependent on white consumerism and black labor for survival in the early decades of the twentieth century, helps to illuminate John Cell's assertion that Jim Crow was more than embedded in local customs or legal practice.[48] Jim Crow was, especially in New South Miami, a particularly complete cultural system rife with rituals and terrorism by vigilantes and police alike, but always embedded in the consumer market and symbiotic to the "Magic City's" real estate and tourism industries. Racial segregation of the labor force, polity, and Miami's housing and tourism industries were symbiotic to the racial segregation celebrated and reified in mass marketing of South Florida. With segregation precluding black patronage at most tourist facilities in

---

[48] Jim Crow was, John Cell argued, essentially a new political system of horizontal oppression that replaced the old vertical one grounded in slavery. See John W. Cell, *The Highest Stage of White Supremacy: The Origins of Segregation in South Africa and the American South* (Cambridge and New York: Cambridge University Press, 1982), 122.

New South cities such as Miami, African Americans were incorporated into southern tourism not as full equals, but as domesticated "others" represented for "public consumption."[49] Nina Silber, in fact, wrote that northerners viewed southern blacks "as simply another feature of the landscape."[50] Her assertions are especially demonstrated in marketing of South Florida, which often depict African Americans and also Seminole Indians as rural, exotic, and impotent social "others" that, as Marguerite Shaffer might argue, helped to reaffirm middleclass white tourists' own sense of refinement, culture, status, urbanity, and Americanness.[51]

Racist ads for South Florida that depict both African Americans and Seminole Indians (a nation comprised of Cherokees who had intermarried with runaway slaves) as inferior and/or part of nature and thus far removed from urbanity were often used to stealth-market the Gold Coast's hotels, attractions, and real estate – the markets of which were segregated by race and class.

But Seminoles' and especially black Miamians' marginal status was not just commodified via mass marketing such as postcards and brochures, it was

---

[49] Fitzhugh W. Brundage, *The Southern Past: A Clash of Race and Memory.* (Cambridge, Mass.: Belknap Press of Harvard University Press, 2005).

[50] Nina Silber, *The Romance of Reunion: Northerners and the South, 1865–1890* (Chapel Hill, UNC Press, 1993), 78.

[51] For more on middleclass white Americans defining themselves through mass consumption in contrast to "social others" (particularly Native Americans) largely barred from the mainstream market, see Marguerite S. Shaffer, *See America First: Tourism and National Identity, 1880-1940* (Washington: Smithsonian Institution Press, 2001), particularly 280.

also performed daily via the city's tourist attractions, and in restaurants and hotels, all of which barred black patronage, yet often hired black servants to tend to the all-white clientele.[52] Part of the luxurious spectacle associated with vacationing in a New South city such as Miami was being almost exclusively tended to by black maids, cooks, waitresses, porters, bellhops, busboys, and rickshaw pullers. A vacation in Miami, in that sense, was comparable to being a slave master in the antebellum era in the American South. In other words, part of the lure of visiting a New South City such as Miami was consuming the fantasy of owning slaves. Images, as well as rituals of consumerism, such as a vacation in a Jim Crow city such as Miami, also served to reify to white Americans what seemed to be their naturally ordained superiority in the nation's racially segregated housing and labor markets. In other words, Miami was crafted to be a place where white supremacy was ritualistic and so deeply embedded in the

---

[52] For secondary literature on the connection between Jim Crow and Indian reservations see: Orlan J. Svingen, "Jim Crow, Indian Style," *American Indian Quarterly*, Vol. 11, No. 4 (Autumn, 1987), pp. 275-286; Jeanette Wolfley, Jim Crow Indian Style: The Disenfranchisement of Native Americans; James R. Bohland, "Indian Residential Segregation in the Urban Southwest: 1970 and 1980. *Social Science Quarterly;* Vol 63, No A. December 1982; and Malinda Maynor Lowery, *Lumbee Indians in the Jim Crow South: Race, Identity, and the Making of a Nation* (Chapel Hill: University of North Carolina Press, 2010). For an interesting examination of Indians participating in consumer culture see Philip J. Deloria, *Indians in Unexpected Places* (Lawrence: University Press of Kansas, 2004). For more on white Americans and Europeans consuming and imbibing Native American cultural motifs in the twentieth century see: P. Deloria's *Playing Indian* (New Haven and London: Yale University Press 1998); Rayna Green, "The Tribe Called Wannabee: Playing Indian in America and Europe," *Folklore*, Vol. 99, No. 1 (1988), pp. 30-55; Robert F. Berkhofer, Jr., *The White Man's Indian: Images of the American Indian from Columbus to the Present* (New York: Alfred A. Knopf, 1978); Gerd Gemünden, "Between Karl May and Karl Marx: The DEFA Indianerfilme (1965-1983)." *New German Critique*, No. 82, East German Film (Winter, 2001), pp. 25-38.

city's industries, culture, and identity that it seemed as if it had always been that way, which, in Miami, it had.

Miami was founded in 1896, more than a generation after the American Civil War (1861–1865). Jim Crow's rise in Miami is thus more peculiar in the "Magic City" than perhaps in any other New South urban-industrial center. Since Miami was so young and new, it was a kind of tabla rasa that could sidestep more traditional patterns of urbanization in more established southern cities such as New Orleans, Atlanta, Charleston, Charlotte, and Nashville. Miami, as such, did not go through the "sorting out" by class, race, and land use that so many other cities in the South did in the decades after the Civil War.

The rise of Jim Crow in Miami, in fact, can be traced directly to the "mother" and "father" of Miami. Julia Tuttle's original land deeds specified the west side of town as the location for factories and for black residences.[53] Miami's local newspapers, which were every bit as much ads for South Florida as the ads analyzed throughout this study, also peculiarly propagated and naturalized Jim Crow. *The Metropolis*, which was owned by Flagler until 1905, for example, unabashedly advocated the mass deportation of blacks from Florida as a proposed solution to the state's social and political woes. Napoleon Bonaparte Broward, Florida's Populist Governor from 1905 to 1909, who was otherwise

---

[53] Dorothy Jenkins Field, "Tracing Overtown's Vernacular Architecture," *The Journal of Decorative and Propaganda Arts*, Vol. 23, Florida Theme Issue (1998), pp. 322–333; 324.

adversarial in many ways to northern industrialists such as Flagler, likewise proposed the mass removal of black Floridians from the state as a means of quelling racial conflict and lynch terror that dissuaded investment in the state's languishing economy and increasingly pushed black southerners north of the Mason-Dixon Line in the early decades of the twentieth century.[54]

Both of Miami's major newspapers, *The Metropolis* and also *The Miami Herald*, which was considered the less progressive of the two, consistently wrote of the social and political inferiority of black South Floridians, and they carried racially degrading stories, which often caricaturized African Americans and Bahamians as "hamfat," "coon," "brute," "fiend," and "darky."[55] In 1897, B.B. Tatum, a Southern Democrat from Georgia, also openly advocated lynching when he editorialized that, "The deplorable circumstances of the assault upon a respectable white woman" (reported in Key West) "by a fiendish black brute," brought "home to us (white Miamians and visitors to the city) the question of what can be done with these black sons of hell." He also encouraged would-be vigilantes to dole out a "necktie party" to the man charged, but not yet convicted, of assailing the accusatory white woman.[56]

---

[54] Samuel Proctor, *Napoleon Bonaparte Broward: Florida's Fighting Democrat* (Gainesville: University of Florida Press, 1950), 37.

[55] *Miami Metropolis*, August 29, 1902, February 27, December 11, 1903, *Miami Daily Metropolis*, April 15, June 5, 1909; *Miami Herald*, October 5, 1911; *Miami Herald*, October 5, 1911, June 2, 1919.

[56] *Miami Metropolis*, Jan. 23, 1903.

The rise of Jim Crow in Miami, in short, skirts the *de jure/de facto* segregation debate because the city was founded by northerners as a racially segregated city in 1896, the same year in which the federal government ultimately sanctioned Jim Crow as a protection of private property rights (*Plessy v. Ferguson*). Miami is also somewhat exceptional from many other Jim Crow cities in the New South, as well as racially segregated cities throughout the Atlantic World, because it, far more than most, desperately depended on white consumers' patronage and black service-industry workers to serve them. Miami's image as a utopian resort city readymade for white consumers deep in the heart of Dixie, as depicted in tandem in racist ads and local newspapers, was deeply connected to the reality of white terrorism and racially segregated housing and labor markets in South Florida. Black laborers – particularly service industry workers and agricultural workers – were, as Melanie Shell-Weiss, Robert Cassanello, and other scholars have helped to illuminate, especially vital to Miami's astounding growth and development in the early decades of the twentieth century.[57]

Black labor was, in short, vital to Miami's meteoric ascendance in the early decades of the twentieth century. But racial segregation was equally vital to the incredible spike in Miami's real estate industry in the early decades of the 1920s.

---

[57] Robert Cassanello and Melanie Shell Weiss, eds. *Florida's Working-Class Past: Current Perspectives on Labor, Race, and Gender from Spanish Florida to the New Immigration* (Gainesville, Fla. University of Florida Press, 2009).

In 1921, the banker-politicians on the Miami City Commission wrote a new city charter granting themselves the power to "establish and set apart" separate residential districts "for white and Negro residents." The charter explicitly prohibited blacks and whites from establishing businesses in districts set aside for the racial other.[58] Jim Crow thus permitted real estate developers to literally dictate the price of land based on how close it was to the bay or beach and how far it was from black sections of the city. A racially divided labor force concomitantly gave city fathers the lion's share of bargaining power amongst both black and white construction workers and service industry workers.

The burden of responsibility for Jim Crow in Miami ultimately lies with socioeconomically-privileged white real estate barons such as Flagler, Tuttle, and newspapermen, as well as the Miami Board of Trade and City Council, and various lobbying groups with the greatest amount of capital invested in the "Magic City's" tourism and real estate industries.[59] White supremacy, in other words, is not exclusively — or even mostly — the product of crude, irrational prejudice concocted in the paranoid minds of ignorant, unskilled white workers

---

[58] N.D.B. Connolly, "Timely innovations: planes, trains and the 'whites only' economy of a Pan-American city," *Urban History*, 36, 2 (2009), pp. 243 – 261, 249.

[59] See Lawrence H. Larsen, *The Rise of the Urban South* (Lexington: University of Kentucky Press, 1985); also see Raymond A. Mohl, *The New City: Urban America in the Industrial Age, 1860–1920* (Arlington Heights, Ill.: Harlan Davidson, Inc., 1985). Mohl argued that "the Right" came to see the municipal corporation both as maintaining social peace and joining with businessmen to bring order to a disorderly free-market economy (pp. 144–47). "The Left" came to see the municipality as an institution of social control, which managed an unruly and socially progressive proletariat (pp. 162–65).

suffering from status anxiety. Jim Crow was prominently packaged and sold by commercial-civic elites, real estate developers, advertisers, medical professionals, and various other people with access to state-of-the-art communication technology, albeit readily consumed by white working– and middleclass consumers, who benefited hand-over-fist from the black second-class citizenship reified in Miami's commodified form specifically, and American consumer culture more generally during the early decades of the twentieth century.

This postcard celebrating the KKK in Miami particularly demonstrates how public and popular the "Invisible Empire" had become in the decade after *Birth of a Nation* debuted, and that Jim Crow in Miami was an especially complete cultural system. The copyright date (1916) on the card is just a year after *Birth of a Nation* was released. "Ku Klux Klan Float," (J.N. Chamberlain, 1916). Historical Association of South Florida, Miami Postcard Collection.

Note how this postcard, with whites ruling Miami's suburban spaces, contrasts with pejorative imagery of black folks and Seminole Indians set in nature (see images below). "Ku Klux Klan Float," (J.N. Chamberlain, 1916). Historical Association of South Florida, Miami Postcard Collection.

Note how this boy is staged in nature with a donkey and surrounded by citrus, one of South Florida's most vital resources and exports to the rest of the nation. Notice how there is, however, no hint of urbanity in the image. "Among the Oranges in Florida," early twentieth century, Florida Historical Society, Cocoa, Ada E. Parrish Postcard Collection, folder: "black."

Much like images of Vizcaya and Flagler hotels helped to imbue value in otherwise frontier and thus mostly valueless land, images depicting minorities as a relic of the past and/or part of nature and far removed from urban space also served to market the ideology of white supremacy in the realm of consumerism, pop culture, and white nationalism. The black boys (above right) are staged adjacent to oranges, as if both were equal parts of the South Florida landscape. "Miami, Jewel of the South," (J.N. Chamberlain, Miami, Fla., 1920), University of Florida Special Collections, Smathers Library, Ephemera collection, folder 44, number 1240.

Seminole Indians and black Floridians were both often depicted as imperiled and/or part of nature, but never urbane. "Seminole Indian Children at Musqisle," early twentieth century, Miami, Florida Historical Society, Cocoa, Ada E. Parrish Postcard Collection, folder: "Seminole."

Both black folks and Seminoles were often staged as helpless children preyed upon by alligators. "An All-in Gator Lunch in Florida," early twentieth century, Florida Historical Society, Cocoa, Ada E. Parrish Postcard Collection, folder: "black.

Black Floridians were often depicted as imperiled by alligators in postcards advertising turn-of-the-century South Florida. Also note the caricatured vernacular in the caption (top right). "A Darky's Prayer," Curt Teich & Co. Inc., early twentieth century, Florida Historical Society, Cocoa, Ada E. Parrish Postcard Collection, folder: "black."

Note the land reclamation billboard juxtaposed with a Seminole Indian, which underscores how Miami was often marketed as a racially coded frontier of capitalism prime for exploitation; Claude C. Matlack, Seminole navigating a canal along the Tamiami Trail. (Tamiami Canal, Fla.), March 27, 1920, Matlack Box 5, number 30, Historical Museum of South Florida.

The black men in this image are employees and the white folks are guests at Henry Flagler's Royal Palm Hotel. Note the Victorian attire of the ladies in contrast to the servile attire worn by the black laborers, which is similar in design to the attire worn by servants in nineteenth century India – the "crown jewel" of the British Empire. Florida photo album Collection, late 19th and early 20th century; Florida Historical Society, Cocoa, Florida.

# Chapter Four

"Masculine Supremacy and Anxiety in Mass Marketing of Miami"

As often as Miami was depicted as a Jim Crow city in the Deep South in which traditional and "proper" racial mores reigned supreme, white women were even more often depicted as objects to be desired and consumed along with the city. Scantily clad white women were often depicted to be both tourist attraction and as synonymous with Miami's image, just as Mickey Mouse is to Disney. Miami's rise, it is important to note, coincided with a robust women's rights movement in northern cities. Images depicting women in Miami as sexualized, sensual and seemingly synonymous with nature speaks to the national anxiety associated with urban-industrialization and its challenge to traditional Judeo-Christian gender norms, which increasingly provided Christian and Jewish women in northern cities new avenues out of the domestic sphere and into public life and politics, which threatened to destroy the suburban sanctity and sanctuary associated with the home as a respite from the urban-industrial dynamo supposedly destroying civilization.

Marketing of Miami often depicted the "Magic City" as a kind of secluded sphere that was as warm, soft, and as inviting as one's home was meant to be. The American garden and the American Dream were gradually and synergistically commoditized as the "Miami Dream" through the objectification of women, who were made synonymous with suburban serenity in the lap of sun, fun, sensuality, and decadent leisure. Ads for Miami that were heavily imbued with notions of social mobility, white supremacist nationalism, Jim Crow, and traditional gender norms thus serve to alert consumers that although Miami was an "instant city" whose economic development was incumbent on a new era of finance capitalism and consumer spectacle, the "Magic City" was ultimately a conservative place in terms of white male privilege and power.

Many men who made Miami into a commodity used the dark art of seduction to sell their product. Mass marketers of Miami were caught up in the same zeitgeist as ad men such as Sigmund Freud's nephew, Edward Bernays, who had, by the end of World War I, mastered the art of manipulating the masses by appealing to consumers' passions – such as fear, anxiety, and sexual desires – rather than their sense of thrift and reason. Miami Beach developer Carl Fisher, for instance, summarized the "Magic City's" most pervasive marketing ethos when he said, "We'll get the prettiest girls we can find and put them in the goddamnedest tightest and shortest bathing suits . . . We'll have their pictures taken and send them all over the goddamn country."[60] The growth of Miami, Jack Kofoed likewise wrote, was "one of the real romances of American business" because "free spenders like liquor, horses, slim legs, pretty faces, gambling and similar amusements… You can't lure them with strawberry

---

[60] Carl Fisher as quoted in Jane Fisher, *Fabulous Hoosier: A Story of American Achievement* (New York: Robert M. McBride and Company, 1947), 149.

festivals and Sunday school picnics."[61] The most prominent way to get the attention of the free-spending men like Fisher and Everett Sewell coveted, was by objectifying women and nature.

Advertisers all over the Atlantic World in the early decades of the twentieth century, used some variant of seaside girls to sell all sorts of things such as soap, ointment, and citrus, and even entire cities such as Miami. One of the "Magic City's" primary draws, like Atlantic City, was that it was along the shore, as well as an exciting, daring, and suburban "open city." Marketing of Miami thus enticed heterosexual bachelors with utopian visions of rows of girls nestled gently in pastoral seaside idylls seemingly beckoning them to South Florida.

In addition to more subtle and sensual objectification of women in promotional material of and about Miami, the "Magic City's" civic elites — like Atlantic City's boosters — also sponsored high-dollar beauty pageants as a means of seducing heterosexual men to Miami.[62] Men also almost never outnumber women in early ads for Miami, thereby creating the spectacle that the

---

[61] Jack Kofoed, "Miami," *The North American Review, Vol. 228, No. 6* (Dec., 1929), pp. 670–673.

[62] see Charles E. Funnell, *By the Beautiful Sea: The Rise and High Times of That Great American Resort, Atlantic City* (New York: Alfred A. Knopf, 1975), 40. See also Sally West, *I Shop in Moscow: Advertising and the Creation of Consumer Culture in Late Tsarist Russia* (DeKalb: Northern Illinois University Press, 2011).

man-to-woman ratio was especially favorable to heterosexual bachelors.[63] Marketers of Miami, in short, consistently depicted the city as young, vibrant, natural, beautiful, active, exuberant, feminine, and often wearing nothing but a bathing suit (and sometimes less than that).

By the 1920s, the objectified women used to market Miami were most often depicted as the "It Girl," "New Woman," or Flapper, replete with short dresses, pouting lips, and bobbed hair, which was also very popular in northern cities and in Hollywood movies at the time.[64] Though Miami was often made synonymous with Old South (i.e. antebellum) iconography in promotional materials, images of the "Magic City" rarely evoked the meek Victorian miss or Scarlett O'Hara character made famous by Margaret Mitchell's *Gone With the Wind* (1936).

Miami's objectified image, however, also opened the city to criticism lobbed from other parts of the country that had lost residents as a result of being seduced to Miami by ads promising consumers social transcendence. Kenneth Roberts, author of a *Saturday Evening Post* series, and subsequent book about Florida, for instance, defended Florida's whorish 1920's boom time reputation by portraying naysayers in Midwestern states such as Ohio and Minnesota as old,

---

[63] See Thomas Richards, *The Commodity Culture of Victorian England: Advertising and Spectacle, 1851–1914* (Palo Alto, Ca., Stanford: Stanford University Press, 1990).

[64] See Barbara Welter, "The Cult of True Womanhood: 1820-1860," *American Quarterly* 18, no. 2 (Summer 1966): 151.

frail, and frightened. These dastardly detractors, Roberts wrote, depicted Florida as a shameless "hussy" and "trollop" similarly to the way women who grew up in the Victorian Era criticized flappers in the 1920s. "Florida is too young and fresh and active for these old and ancient Northern states," Roberts wrote, "and she fills them with suspicion and distrust."[65] But what Roberts overlooked was that Miami was, in fact, designed to elicit such visceral reactions. Boosters did not think of Miami's sultry, seductive, and feminized image as a bad thing, but rather as a dire necessity to get the attention of, and ultimately lure, free spenders, especially heterosexual men, to South Florida by any means necessary.

Miami has, as the ads analyzed throughout this study help to illuminate, always been as much a concocted brand readymade for consumption as much as an actual place in southeast Florida. Part of the reason for the preeminence of Miami's image to its urbanization is that South Florida's rise coincided with the popularization of industrialized communication technologies such as sheet music, phonographs, and cinema, as well as seductive print ads in magazines that were routinely distributed throughout the world. All these technologies were synergistic to Miami's urbanization. And what is especially instructive is that all these communication technologies often had one thing in common: the

---

[65] Kenneth L. Roberts, *Florida* (New York: Harper and Brothers Publishers, 1926), 323–324. See also, Nicole C. Cox, "Selling Seduction: Women and Feminine Nature in 1920s Florida Advertising," *Florida Historical Quarterly,* Fall 2010 Vol. 89 No. 2. 193.

depiction of South Florida, especially Miami, as a consumer's utopia. American utopianism was thoroughly sexualized to address the masculine anxiety associated with women's economic and political mobility.

Popular musicians of the era conspicuously championed Miami as a joyous consumerist fantasy subsequent to vitally crafting the romance and sensuality (real and/or imagined) of the "Magic City." In 1925, for instance, Al Jolson crooned, "My Miami, you belong to me, my flowers, my land, my birdies, too; Miami, take your sonny to your sunny clime! Miami, tell me honey, I'll be there on time."[66] Charles Bayha likewise titillated listeners with ditties such as "Old Honolulu has beaches it's true, where all the girls wicky wacky and woo. But on our beaches that's not half what they do — I'd rather be in Miami," thereby evoking the notion that girls in Miami were especially adventurous, if not licentious.[67]

The incredibly popular and powerful new medium of cinema also especially produced the notion of Miami as a spectacle and fantasy waiting to be fulfilled for heterosexual men with money (or at least access to consumer credit).

---

[66] William E. Brown, Jr., "Pan Am: Miami's Wings to the World," *The Journal of Decorative and Propaganda Arts*, Vol. 23, Florida Theme Issue (1998), pp. 144–161.

[67] Caesar LaMonica, "Miami: of the U.S.A.!" Playground (New York, 1925); Charles Bayha, "I'd Rather Be in Miami"(Coral Gables, Fla.,1927); R. H. Bonnell, "Mi-Ami-My Lady-My Miami By the Sea," (NewYork,1925); Alice Sparks, "The Magic Realm" (Miami, Fla., 1928); See sheet music collection of the Historical association of Southern Florida and Florida State Archives.

The silent film, *Miami* (1924), which was directed by Max Gluckman and produced by the Miami City Council, was advertised as a "Jazz Movie" chocked full of sex, sensuality, "spice and spectacle." But more than anything, the movie was a commercial to market Miami to the world beyond Biscayne Bay. The film is a particularly great example of how seemingly progressive, but in truth conservative, gender norms could be in the realm of Roaring Twenties popular culture.

The synopsis is as follows: The protagonist, Joan Bruce (Betty Compson), a caricature of a Flapper/New Woman, is "a girl whose only thought [is] the mad pursuit of pleasure and thrills and the conquest of the other sex." She pursues Grant North (Benjamin F. Finney, Jr.) – a wealthy northerner who is a kind of caricature of a Yankee real estate baron – who, much to Joan's consternation, refuses to have anything to do with her due to how unladylike she acts (such as jumping in a pool naked). But when she gets in a motorboat accident, North chivalrously rescues her, and their romance blooms. But when he leaves Miami on a short business trip, their relationship is imperiled by her promiscuity. Though Joan has sworn to be faithful to her new beau, she is lured to a yacht belonging to a local (i.e. southern) bootlegger named Ranson Tate (Lawford Davidson). The pair leaves town soon after their affair begins, which, due to Tate's marital status, causes a scandalous stir amongst the locals. North, however, ardently believes that Joan truly loves him. So he, along with his trusted associate, Colonel David Forbes (J. Barney Sherry), chases after her and Tate. Joan and Tate quarrel on his boat. Tate is primed to violently attack Joan just as North arrives in time to save the damsel in distress. North ultimately, though reluctantly, forgives Joan's betrayal after she essentially vows to be more ladylike and his kept woman. They presumably live happily ever after in Miami.

On the surface, the film seems to evoke the power and spectacle of the "New Woman," but ultimately leads to the damsel in distress learning the hard way that she is far better off living the life of a Victorian era housewife (a bird in a Gilded Cage) than as a libertine New Woman. In *Miami* (the movie), which was produced to seduce consumers to South Florida, there is still an underlying Darwinist ethos in which urban space is a kind of modernized jungle in which men are violent and women need protection. What is perhaps most instructive about *Miami,* the movie, music, and print ads regaling the "Magic City" as a seductive site of social transcendence and proper racial and gender norms is how these sources unabashedly celebrate South Florida's "open" reputation – replete with fast women, booze, gambling, nightlife, sin, sex, and seduction – and yet ironically evoke women's reliance on men for protection, and especially for access to the consumer market.

Gendered ads for Miami also betray an attempt by boosters to reconcile the popularity of the supposedly progressive "New Woman's" commoditized form with traditional gender norms as a means of selling the "Magic City" to both progressive and conservative consumers.[68] For example, though Miami's image was often depicted to be white and feminine, women were thoroughly objectified, thereby creating the notion that Miami was a man's city where traditional Judeo-Christian gender norms ultimately reigned supreme. And, although many women in ads of Miami evoke the "New Woman" (i.e. modern) motif replete with short dresses or bathing suits, bobbed hair, and rouged cheeks, it was, as *Miami* the movie particularly illuminates, used by marketers of Miami to serve consumerism and thus to serve conservative ends.

Although women were often depicted ornamentally, women consuming ads for Miami, and vacationing in the "Magic City," were concomitantly being instructed on how to perform as consumers in the context of an ever-evolving and global commercial empire. In the marketing of Miami, the focus for women's consumption was often paradoxical. For instance, women were staged as objects to be desired, conquered, and consumed, but also often staged as maternal objects. In many ads for Miami, women's roles were often varied around acts of leisure such as dining, shopping, sunbathing, or golfing, but also sometimes domestic in focus. Some brochures even depict what seem to be single women engaged in idle luxury on a beach or golf course, but when the brochure is folded

---

[68] For more on the display of women and men in the interest of portraying empire and nation, see Victoria De Grazia and Ellen Furlough, eds, *The Sex of Things: Gender and Consumption in Historical Perspective* (University of California Press, 1996). See also John Tosh, *A Man's Place: Masculinity and the Middle-Class Home in Victorian England* (New Haven, CT and London: Yale University Press, 1999).

open, the women are conspicuously displayed with children. Women are also often depicted in ads of Miami as sunbathing with their kids, or perhaps viewed by female consumers of the material as nannies babysitting their children. Either way, women were often displayed as decorative objects imbued with class designators designed to lure both male and female consumers to Miami concomitant to instructing them on how to be modern consumers, which was increasingly conflated with American identity.[69]

The pervasive objectification of women depicted in Miami's commoditized form adds new depth to Thornstein Veblen's *Theory of the Leisure Class: An Economic Study in the Evolution of Institutions* (1899). Veblen established a theory of consumer culture around an ironic anthropology of rivalry and display in which sexual distinctions were central, with the "conspicuous" consumption of bourgeois men being displayed vicariously in their wives' clothes, jewels, pale skin, and leisure activities.[70] But gendered ads of Miami also indicate that by feminizing the city's image, the men responsible for mass marketing their product (the "Magic City") and interests (tourism/real estate industry) ultimately articulated the city's identity in the realm of consumerism as

---

[69] For more on the display of the family unit in mass marketing, see Roland Marchand, *Advertising the American Dream: Making Way for Modernity, 1920–1940* (Berkeley: University of California Press, 1985).

[70] Thornstein Veblen, *Theory of the Leisure Class: An Economic Study in the Evolution of Institutions* (New York: Macmillan, 1899).

a hegemonic white masculine sphere of socioeconomic and political privilege and domination. In many early ads for Miami, men, in stark contrast to women, were narrowly cast as businessmen or upwardly mobile idlers, and women — even those depicted as "New Women" — were often depicted to be happy homemakers or part of the landscape to be conquered and exploited. Miami was, in short, crafted to be a man's city via conspicuously mass marketing white women as happy consumers in the lap of luxury.

Thus, in spite of what seemed to be a glaring paradox in the marketing of Miami, the ads depicted in this chapter actually perpetuated a traditional gendered and heteronormative vision of social amelioration via Miami's commoditized form that ultimately depended on adherence to the white male authority part and parcel of global capitalism in the twentieth century.

In short, the propagators of Miami's urbanization, like turn-of-the-century American business leaders, increasingly pointed consumers toward the world of commodities — particularly in cities such as Miami — for their direction. Miami's civic elites, like Corporate America in general, increasingly sold consumers on the idea that the market was "the father of us all" by increasingly and pervasively appealing to men's libidinal and domesticated desires by conspicuously objectifying women as sexual and maternal objects.

Many women also bought into the traditional gender norms being sold along with Miami, and, since consumers targeted by ads of Miami would have just as likely been bourgeois women at home checking the mail or reading *McClure's Magazine* as they would have been consumed by businessmen reading *The Wall Street Journal*, the image of feminized luxury that was part of Miami's commodified form was one that showed female consumers that the impression of a leisured lifestyle was integral to her position in the urban-industrial social hierarchy.[71] In other words, stereotypes acted as prototypes of a shared cultural meaning that arose through representational simplicity, immediate reconcilability, and implicit reference to assumed consensus about idealized white femininity.[72] This especially included consuming the notion that white women's proper place in the social hierarchy was naturally in the private sphere and dependent on white men for protection and access to the consumer market.[73]

Miami was thus marketed as a gendered tonic to northern urbanization and industrialization, which increasingly lured women out of the domestic sphere and put them in competition with men for opportunities, resources, and control of both urban spaces and the private home. As such, a romanticized view of feminine nature, coupled with white female consumers engaged in idle luxury, increasingly encouraged middleclass American men and women to

---

[71] Monica Neve, *Sold! Advertising and the Bourgeois Female Consumer in Munich, 1900-1914* (Stuttgart: Franz Steiner Verlag, 2010), 113.

[72] Carolyn Kitch, *The Girl on the Magazine Cover: The Origins of Visual Stereotypes in American Mass Media* (Chapel Hill, University of North Carolina Press, 2001), 5.

[73] Stuart Ewen, *Captains of Consciousness: Advertising and the Social Roots of the Consumer Culture* (New York: McGraw-Hill, 1976), 56, 85, 86, 91, 109 and 184.

escape the noise, filth, disease, grime, crime, and threat to traditional gender and racial mores in more established cities for the fresh air, natural environment, and conservatism of new suburban oasis such as Miami. The water, sunshine, implicitly available young white women, and fresh air of the Atlantic Ocean hailed in the marketing of Miami, all served — promotional brochures suggested — as a redemptive agent for the tainted atmosphere of industrialized cities north of the Mason-Dixon Line. Miami thus fused the promise of amoral excitement with the restorative and healthful effects of sunshine and salt water as a kind of redemptive and regenerative baptismal font and fountain of youth for old and young saints and sinners alike.[74]

"Capital is," as William Cronon wrote, "created by an act of perception, by seeing in a certain way."[75] Thanks in part to gendered ads of the city, and its "virgin" lands, Miami's marketers helped to demonstrate how first-nature was, in the early twentieth century, gradually rearranged into commodities — resorts, hotel rooms, plots of land, houses, gated communities, department stores, shopping centers, stadiums, and oceanfront property — within the second nature of the capitalist market. What has often overlooked, however, in the role that ads

---

[74] For more on the paradox between a sinful city nestled next to the redemptive sea, see E. Funnell, *By the Beautiful Sea*.

[75] For more on the relationship between city and hinterland and the transformation of "first nature" into "second nature," see William Cronon, *Nature's Metropolis: Chicago and the Great West* (New York: Norton, 1991), especially 265–266.

played in transforming first-nature into second-nature, was that those ads often defined second-nature as feminine and white. Miami's urbanization, and the industrialization of tourism and real estate so essential to the "Magic City's" rise, was thus most often associated with iconography depicting women as one with nature and the embodiment of fecundity, rebirth, and nurturance. This was especially evident in the creation myth of the cornucopia that was sometimes used to market frontier South Florida.[76] As such, a feminized view of nature was ironically central to Miami's image and subsequent suburban-industrial development through the 1920s.

Guidebooks, like promotional brochures, lured tourists to scenic rivers, beaches, and swamps, but also instructed tourists on how to comport themselves as consumers in a freewheeling "open city" such as Miami. Guidebooks and brochures, Dona Brown writes, "celebrated seeing nature as separate from and superior to the vulgarities of urban commerce and industry."[77] In Miami, however, the celebration of nature was central to the vulgarities of commerce

---

[76] Mary Louise Roberts, "Gender, Consumption, and Commodity Culture," *The American Historical Review*, Vol. 103, No. 3 (Jun., 1998), pp. 817–844, 829; For more on the treatment of women as visual and verbal symbols, see also Jackson Lears, *Fables of Abundance* (New York: Basic Books, 1994); and also Martha Banta, *Imaging American Women: Idea and Ideals in Cultural History* (New York: Columbia University Press, 1987).

[77] For more on tourist brochures instructing consumers on how to react to the wonders of nature, see Dona Brown, *Inventing New England: Regional Tourism in the Nineteenth Century* (Washington, D.C.: Smithsonian Institution Press, 1995); and also Nicholas Green, *The Spectacle of Nature: Landscape and Bourgeois Culture in Nineteenth-Century France* (New York, St. Martin's Press, 1990); Green argues that the appropriation of nature renders it an object of consumption.

and industry. The feminine nature iconography associated with the "Magic City" and Florida writ large was marketed as a kind of antidote to masculine Taylorist industrialization associated with turn-of-the century cities such as Boston, Cleveland, Philadelphia, Chicago, New York, London, Liverpool, Manchester, and especially the stark deprivation associated with the Soviet Union.[78]

In fact, while many Atlantic World cities were often depicted to be both masculine, polluted, and in decay by the time Miami was incorporated in 1896, the "Magic City" was conspicuously marketed as feminine and often maternal as a means of attracting homeseekers with a cult of domesticity iconography. As such, a romanticized view of feminine nature, coupled with white female consumers engaged in idle leisure in the lap of luxury, increasingly encouraged middleclass American men and women to escape the social decay associated with northern cities for the fresh air and natural (suburban) environment imbued in early advertising of Miami.

The conflation of sun, sex, salvation, fun, excitement, and good health in Miami's commoditized form was especially powerful in luring retirees (i.e. people who grew up or came of age in the Victorian Era and Gilded Age) to

---

[78] For more on Southern California defining itself as an anecdote to eastern urbanization, see Clark Davis, "From Oasis to Metropolis: Southern California and the Changing Context of American Leisure," *Pacific Historical Review*, Vol. 61, No. 3 (May, 1992), pp. 357–386. For a short but useful comparison of Miami and Los Angeles, see William Deverell, Greg Hise and David C. Sloane, "Orange Empires: Comparing Miami and Los Angeles," *Pacific Historical Review*, Vol. 68, No. 2, Orange Empires (May, 1999), pp. 145–152.

Miami. One of the primary tropes evident in the marketing of first-generation Miami, in fact, evoked Florida's founding by the Spanish Empire in the sixteenth century, most notably Ponce de Leon's quest to find the mythic fountain of youth. Miami Beach developer Carl Fisher likewise marketed his suburb as a place where "the old could grow young and the young never grow old." Henry Flagler, who died in 1913, "lived," according to F. Page Wilson, "long enough to look on Miami as the 'City of Eternal Youth.'"[79] Eternal youth and beauty was, of course, something not even Flagler could buy, but he and many others could sure as hell sell it. So much so that by World War I, South Florida was increasingly synonymous with youthful exuberance.[80]

In glaring contrast to the depiction in ads of Miami, the city's boosters often cast themselves in the dominant role as community builders (i.e. civilizers), remaking and improving a feminine nature to achieve their goals of "progress" (i.e. material prosperity). "For hundreds of years Florida had lain barren, peopled only by a few breech-clothed savages," an ad explained. Now, "men of genius and enterprise at whose magic touch Florida awakened to fulfill *her*

---

[79] F. Page Wilson, "Miami: From Frontier to Metropolis: An Appraisal," *Tequesta*, No. 15, 1955, 34.

[80] As innocuous as making Miami synonymous to youth may seem, the idealization of youth in mass marketing in general, Stuart Ewen argues, enabled business leaders throughout the U.S. to undermine the productive power and skills of more seasoned workers and to "accept malleability, endurance and individualism as positive values" useful for the promotion of consumption; see Ewen's *Captains of Consciousness*, 146.

destiny" had transformed a frontier into markets, value, and profits waiting to be exploited.[81]

Boosters even gendered Miami's weather. Climate was, Victor Rainbolt wrote, a key asset for South Florida's development, and may have been as "tangible in its value as the products of mine or field." He likewise compared leaving Miami to the soft conclusion of a tepid summer day: "We remember only *her* sweetness, the outdoor joy *she* brought us, the crimson of *her* sunsets, the rose of *her* sunrises, the breath of *her* flowers, the song of *her* birds — the warmth of *her* sun!"[82] Ads likewise often regaled readers with dreams of virgin markets such as: "if investor, here opportunity is blazing manifold for those who seek *her*."[83] Women were also often depicted and referred to as "mermaids" in promotional materials, indicating they were half human and half nature, as if to remind men of their Biblically ordained dominion over both.

In the early decades of the twentieth century, as the pages above illuminate, the American consumer market was as gendered as it was racialized. The home, for example, was still widely considered the private sphere and a feminine domain to foster children and provide a haven for men forced to

---

[81] See Raymond B. Vickers, "Addison Mizner: Promoter in Paradise," *The Florida Historical Quarterly*, Vol. 75, No. 4 (Spring, 1997), pp. 381–407.

[82] Victor Rainbolt, *The Town That Climate Built: The Story of the Rise of a City in the American Tropics* (Miami, FL: Parker Art Printing Association, 1925), 133–136.

[83] "Miami by-the-Sea," (Miami Chamber of Commerce, Miami, Fla., 1922).

confront the harsh drudgery of an increasingly competitive urban-industrial society. The industrial city was often thought of as a Social Darwinian masculine sphere where only the fittest of survivors could thrive. The city was most prominently the place where working class men competed for better wages and concessions against capitalists, middle managers, and other workers desperate to survive. Cities were also increasingly divided into racial and ethnic enclaves, such as "Colored Town" and "Lemon City," where black Miamians were largely confined, in contrast to Miami Beach, which barred all but the wealthiest white families. The city was thus considered the antithesis of the home. The more dystopian the industrial city became during the Gilded Age, the more utopian marketing of "instant cities" such as Miami were conspicuously depicted to be.

As essential as mass marketing was to imbuing value in the South Florida frontier in the early decades of the Gold Coast's urbanization, Miami's image ultimately betrays deep uneasiness and anxiety in reaction to the rapid transition of the United States from an agrarian backwater to the world's premier commercial and military power. The gendering of ads so prominent in Miami's commoditized form were thus not just selling the city, its attractions, amenities, and real estate; the ads also explicitly sold the image and idea of white masculine supremacy of urban spaces (including private homes) and, by implication, the global economy, which was increasingly fueled by mass consumption of "modern" luxuries such as vacations, automobiles, household appliances, as well as racially segregated urban property and labor markets.

WHERE HAPPINESS IS UNCONFINED

The picture above depicts one man flanked by eighteen women in bathing suits. The row of implicitly available white women pervasively depicted in marketing of Miami was popular throughout the Atlantic World, especially resort cities such as Miami. "Miami Beach is Calling You to the Tropics," (Miami Beach Chamber of Commerce, early 1920s), Smathers Library Special Collections, Ephemera Collection, University of Florida. Folder 39, number 1118.

*Sun-ray prescriptions — just what the doctor ordered.*

Note how even when climate and sun is being sold as prescriptive, the female form is what is intended to draw the viewer's gaze in this brochure marketing Miami. "Outdoor Sports Capital of America," Miami Beach Chamber of Commerce, Florida Historical Society, Cocoa, PAM Collection, Box 11, Folder 3.

The photos above are found in a brochure in which every image depicts women in bathing suits. As such, white women are being marketed as much as the city's sites and amenities. Such pervasive use of white women would have been considered pornographic a generation earlier, especially in the Deep South. "Miami By the Sea: The City of Happiness in the State of Florida," (Miami Chamber of Commerce, 1927); Smathers Library Special Collections, Ephemera Collection, University of Florida. Folder 39, number 1120.

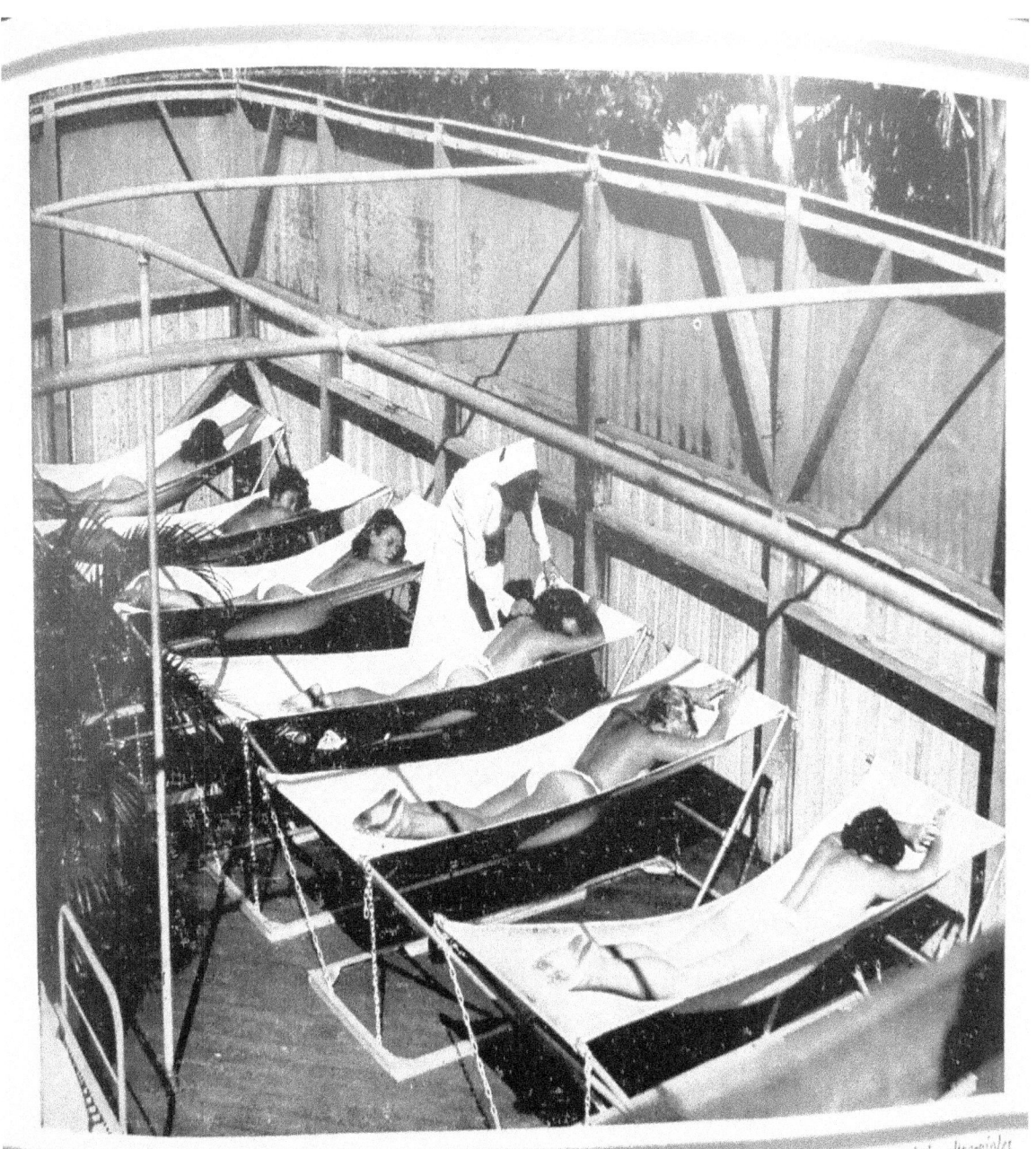

*Medical authorities take advantage of the ultra-violet sunlight to prescribe nude sunbathing for many ailments*

## Sun Ray Prescriptions

The image above uses discourse of health mixed with imagery of topless girls in a row sunbathing to sell Miami to consumers suffering northern winters. "Outwitting Winter: Cities of the Sun, Miami and Miami Beach," Chamber of Commerce, late-1920s, Florida Historical Society, Cocoa, PAM Collection, Box 6, folder 7.

The image above seems to foreshadow Marilyn Monroe in *The Seven Year Itch* (1955), as if the wind might blow up the young woman's dress, which demonstrates how drastically social mores seemed to shift in and through consumer culture from the time of Miami's incorporation in 1896 through the "Roaring Twenties." The text below the image is especially utopian in its description of Miami as the "Perfect City." The ad is also instructive because it promotes the newly built causeway from the mainland to barrier islands, and subsequent emerging secluded/high-end gated communities (and exorbitant property values). "Miami by the Sea: The Land of Palms and Sunshine," Miami Chamber of Commerce (St. Augustine, Florida, The Record Company, 1924); Special Collections, University of Florida, Smathers Library Ephemera Collection, folder 38, number 1106.

This image depicts two presumably single white women engaged in idle leisure. At left, white folks enjoy golf, a game popularized and imported to the United States from Scotland by industrialists such as Andrew Carnegie. The young woman at right has her skirt hiked up way past her knees and appears to be drawing the viewer's gaze towards her vagina with her right hand. Also note the Mediterranean design of the architectural forms in the background, as if to indicate that Miami is European. "Miami by the Sea, The Land of Palms and Sunshine," Miami Chamber of Commerce (St. Augustine, Florida, The Record Company, 1925); Special Collections, University of Florida, Smathers Library Ephemera Collection, folder 38, number 1111.

The image above is particularly interesting because it blends urban nightlife, travel technology, a city skyline, nature, and rollicking Flappers. Note also the class designators of affluent leisure such as men playing tennis and women playing golf. The text below the image, per usual, depicts Miami as a consumerist utopia. "Miami By the Sea: The City of Happiness in the State of Florida," (Miami Chamber of Commerce, 1927); Smathers Library Special Collections, Ephemera Collection, University of Florida. Folder 39, number 1120.

This 1917 brochure shows what is a presumably a mother donning Victorian garb leading what is presumably her children past two men toting golf clubs. By the 1920s, brochures marketing Miami increasingly depicted "New Women" on the adjacent flap of the brochure from children (see images below), thereby insinuating to female consumers that they could have it both ways – utopian consumerist freedom along with family. "Miami By the Sea: The Land of Palms and Sunshine," 1917, page 1. University of Miami Library, Special Collections, ASC9999 F319.M6 M6227 1917.

Some of the most interesting brochures marketing Miami depict what seem to be single women enjoying leisure time. But when folded open, the brochure depicts women with children. Note also the conflation of women, nature, travel technology, and the American flag at the shoreline. The text at lower right depicts Miami as a modern consumerist utopia. "Miami by the Sea," (Miami Chamber of Commerce, Miami, Florida, 1919) 3, Special Collections, University of Florida, Smathers Library Ephemera Collection, folder 37, number 1066.

Note how the woman above (presumably the mother or nanny of the children) is particularly crafted to look like Aryan iconography popular in Weimer Germany and later in Third Reich Germany. The woman and children are also conflated with Dixie. The woman is also objectified to like a hood ornament (i.e. object). "Dixie Route to Florida," Smathers Library, Special Collections, Ephemera Collection, University of Florida; Folder 26, number 2578.

This brochure for Miami Beach displays an Aryan-looking woman that may or may not be the mother of the child on the adjacent side. Here, Miami is constructed to be a feminized bastion of good health and happiness (for white folks). "Miami Beach is Calling You to the Tropics," (Miami Beach Chamber of Commerce, late teens or early 1920s).

Notice how the buxom blond in black bathing suit (at right) is central to the brochure in contrast to how men's bodies are obscured to convey more modesty. Also note the blue-suited businessman at left smoking his pipe gazing longingly at the idyll. The yellow circle at right promises "youth" and "happiness" as synonymous with life in Florida. Note also the conflation of Florida with other northern and southern cities into a national consumer market. "Florida Via the Dixie Route," (Lightfoot Publishing, late 1920s); Smathers Library Special Collections, Ephemera Collection, University of Florida; folder 26, number 2574.

This image was designed to sell citrus and agricultural lands in South and Central Florida. Note the fecund nature, the utopian (and phallic) horn of plenty and cornucopia, all associated with white women skinny-dipping in what is presumably a South Florida river or seaside idyll. "Florida Invites You," (Florida Growers Press, 1927). University of Florida, Smathers Special Collections, Ephemera collection, P.K. Yonge Library of Florida History.

Inside this brochure, young contortionists, and other implicitly available collections of women, beckon consumers to Miami. Many of the girls in the brochure, including the girl in this picture, look younger than 18 years old. "Miami: Golden Sunshine Adds Golden Years," (Hollywood Press, Miami, Fla. 1927); Smathers Library Special Collections, Ephemera Collection, University of Florida. Folder 39, number 1121.

This apartment guide creates the illusion that the female-to-male ratio in post-boom Miami was three-to-one. Note the flapper motif of the women, and the travel technology, including the luxurious sedan. The caption also quotes a founder of John Hopkins University, who states that Florida is a healthy alternative to polluted northern cities. "Miami, Florida Apartments," (Hefty Press, late 1920s/early 1930s); Smathers Special Collections, University of Florida, Ephemera Collection, folder 39, number 1128.

ABOVE: *Rollicking mermaids of the Surf at Miami Beach.*

Rows of scantily clad white women are especially common in marketing of Miami, as is the reference to mermaids. "Outwitting Winter: Cities of the Sun, Miami and Miami Beach," Chamber of Commerce, late-1920s, Florida Historical Society, Cocoa, PAM Collection, Box 6, folder 7.

*A group of young Amazons at a cabana pool gives a fair idea of the results of living in this healthful climate*

## Mermaids and Mere Men

❡Ocean and surf bathing here find a worthy rival in the many picturesque, well-equipped pools of the area. Water sports attract thousands of spectators when Olympic and National aquatic champions compete in weekly exhibitions during the season. Two of the greatest women divers in history, Miss Georgia Coleman and Miss Helen Meany, as well as Johnny Weismuller, Dick Degener, Miss Katherine Rawls and Miss Lenore Kight have startled the blase winter visitors with their feats of skill both in and above the water. Of course, there are stunt competitions like canoe tilting, sliding the greased pole and other aquatic events while fashion shows and beauty contests enliven the hotel and casino pools. Whether you're a mermaid or a mere man, you'll enjoy this modern version of the "Old Swimmin' Hole".

The page above found in a brochure marketing Miami refers to women as both "mermaids" and "Amazons," which is instructive because it conflates femininity with nature as it exhibits the popular motif of collections of seaside girls used to market resort cities in the early decades of the twentieth century. "Outwitting Winter: Cities of the Sun, Miami and Miami Beach," Chamber of Commerce, late-1920s, Florida Historical Society, Cocoa, PAM Collection, Box 6, folder 7.

The blending of "New Women" in bathing suits embossed with tennis racket, golf gear, and a Marlin insinuates that women are game and/or sport in Miami. "Miami By the Sea, The Land of Palms and Sunshine," Miami Chamber of Commerce, 1926, page 25. University of Miami Library, Special Collections, ASC9999 F319.M6 M6227 1926.

ABOVE: *Hula maidens at Tahiti Beach, near Miami.*

The image above of a row of exotic Hula Maidens at Tahiti Beach ("near Miami") illuminates how global the tourism industry so central to Miami's existence, growth and prosperity had already become by the 1920s. The image also helps connect the rise of consumerism with the New Woman motif and more explicit and common objectification of white women in advertising in the decades after the Victorian Era. The lack of modesty exhibited in 1920s advertising is likely reactionary to the confining propriety of the Victorian Era. "Outdoor Sports Capital of America," Miami Beach Chamber of Commerce, Florida Historical Society, Cocoa, PAM Collection, Box 11, Folder 3.

Note how this postcard of William Jennings Bryan (at left) delivering Sunday afternoon sermon in the bandshell on the lawn of the Henry Flagler's Royal Palm Hotel exhibits an overwhelming majority of men in the audience who seem to holistically blend into the swaying palm trees adjacent to the bandshell. Especially note the drab clothing, colors, and modesty of men in contrast to the depiction of women in this study. This is one of the few images marketing Miami that depict white men (who tend to personify urbanity) as the predominant gender in Miami. Women are most often depicted as synonymous with nature and vastly outnumbering men. Pictorial Centre Publishing, Image Courtesy of Florida International University Digital Collection, vintage postcard collection, circa 1910 – 1923, Image number FI05112117.

# Chapter Five

## "Capitalism and Class Anxiety in Mass Marketing of Miami"

Since Miami was so remote and wild, early advertising of the city often accentuated what seemed to be a detriment — distance — as a prime marketing ploy to lure wealthy clientele anxious to escape the urban-industrial dynamo for entire seasons at a time. Rail and real estate barons such as Henry Flagler built a string of coastal hotels for an elite clientele, and a variety of writers wrote and sold guidebooks to promote the region's resorts and attractions. Miami was but one "Magic City" made into a haven south of the Mason-Dixon Line during the Gilded Age and Progressive Era. Flagler and a cadre of industrialists such as J.P. Rockefeller and Cornelius Vanderbilt, who were often aided by the federal government, collectively created an extensive North American "pleasure periphery" comprised of seasonal resorts that dramatically reshaped local economies and landscapes across the eastern seaboard and which, decades later, would become the Sunbelt.

Wealthy entrepreneurs such as Flagler, Vanderbilt, and Addison Mizner often conspicuously imbued value in products or properties they endorsed. This tactic was becoming increasingly commonplace throughout the industrialized world and throughout the twentieth century. Roland Marchand, for instance, highlighted an ad for Pond's Soap endorsed by women of the Vanderbilt, Morgan, Astor, Belmont, Drexel, and du Pont families. These kinds of testimonials of products endorsed by social "elites" often encouraged less affluent consumers to believe that they could ensconce themselves in the same aura of wealth and luxury by purchasing simple household items, or by taking a vacation to a resort city such as Miami, which was conspicuously marketed to be synonymous with wealth and luxury. Celebrity endorsements were likewise prominent in marketing of Miami in the early decades of the twentieth century. Industrialists, civic leaders, movie stars, famous athletes, politicians, and gangsters all spent winters in Miami. Local and national newspapers and sundry other promotional materials meanwhile incessantly hailed elites' interest in South Florida, thereby imbuing "value" in Miami via branding and mass marketing of celebrity/pop culture, which initiated an aesthetic of spectacle and class imitation that helped fuel tourism and real speculation.[84]

Promotional brochures of Miami often celebrated the upper class' conspicuous demarcation from lower classes, but also, concomitantly, helped to naturalize consumers, regardless of class, into a common rubric, thus fostering a more blurred distinction of class identity, providing increasingly socially mobile blue-collar workers with access to consumer credit visions and goals of material prosperity, luxury, and comfort so contrary to the nineteenth-century working-class consciousness illuminated by E.P. Thompson.[85]

---

[84] See Roland Marchand, *Creating the Corporate Soul: The Rise of Public Relations and Corporate Imagery in American Big Business* (Berkeley: University of California Press, 1998).

[85] E. P. Thompson, *The Making of the English Working Class* (London, Pelican, 1963).

Though Miami was founded as an elite retreat catering to Flagler and his ilk, by the 1920s, this image of high society was incessantly used to lure middle- and working-class Americans with access to consumer credit to South Florida with promises of social mobility. By the 1920s, the abundance of wealth in cold northern cities, and the sophisticated travel infrastructure, advertising industry, and climate of South Florida all synergistically helped to transform the frontier into a major vacation destination for people of all classes. The more tourists and homeseekers were lured to the Gold Coast, the more black and white workers also arrived in the city looking for work.

The more consumerist modern America became, the more advertisers sought to exploit workers' revulsion to labor. Jacques Ranciere argued that laborers took little pride in their craft, and despised the discipline, boredom, and servitude of their work. They, Ranciere noted, longed for nights after a long day in the factory during which they could read, write, drink, sing, dance, and thereby achieve an aestheticized release from the grinding hardship of daily life. Though Ranciere's study focused on French workers in the nineteenth century, Ralph Waldo Emerson believed revulsion to labor was also characteristically American. Toil was, Emerson believed, synonymous with slavery and thus contrary to "enlightened" notions of American democracy. Leisure and democracy were often conflated with consumerism, which became king in the early decades of the twentieth century. Marketers of Miami often shrewdly manipulated workers' revulsion to labor and class subjugation by hustling social mobility packaged as speculation, which essentially amounts to gambling. Despite the risk of speculation in a frontier turned burgeoning market, many new arrivals to the "Magic City" were often so seduced by utopian ads of Miami that insinuated social mobility that they often only needed to be shown where and how parcels of land could be quickly acquired.[86]

The best way to exploit South Florida, real estate developer Addison Mizner believed, was to appeal to consumers' sense of class-consciousness. Get the big snobs," he said, "and the little snobs will follow."[87] On April 15, 1925, near the zenith of the South Florida speculative frenzy, Mizner's corporation announced, the development of Boca Raton, which was marketed as the "social capital of the south," and "Venice of the Atlantic."[88] The city was to be "an aristocracy of sport," featuring a thousand-room hotel, two golf courses, a polo field, palatial parks, tennis courts, private beaches, an airport, a marina to house yachts cruising through twenty miles of "lazy lagoons," miles of paved and landscaped streets, which included a 160-foot-wide grand boulevard called Camino Real modeled on the Botofogo in Brazil, a cabaret run by composer

---

[86] Kenneth J. Ballinger, *Miami Millions: The Dance of the Dollars in the Great Florida Land Boom of 1925* (Miami, FL: Printed by The Franklin, 1936), 135 and 141.

[87] "Wilson Mizner: Now We See Him," *Orlando Sentinel Florida Magazine*, January 14, 1973; and Raymond B. Vickers, "Addison Mizner: Promoter in Paradise," *The Florida Historical Quarterly*, Vol. 75, No. 4 (Spring, 1997), pp. 381–407; p. 383.

[88] *Palm Beach Post*, April 15, September 1, 1925, February 26, July 14, 1926; *Boca Raton: Florida's Wholly New Entirely Beautiful World Resort*, MDC Files; Donald W. Curl, "Boca Raton and the Florida Land Boom of the 1920s," *Tequesta*, No. XLVI, 1986, 138–45.

Irving Berlin, and a grand casino (even though casino gambling was technically illegal in Florida).[89] By the time Mizner's syndicate made its first reservation for the purchase of land on May 14, 1925, publicity in the *Palm Beach Post* — a mouthpiece for Mizner interests — announced that the company's stockholders represented more than a third of the entire wealth of the United States. Mizner's advertisements promised that every purchaser of the first day's offering would make quick and large profits. When interviewed by the *Palm Beach Post*, Mizner explained that the $7,000,000 in lots, and $4,000,000 in acreage, sold by the company in fewer than three months "proved the viability" of his vision and enterprise, and that "Boca Raton would stand as a cornerstone to American architectural prestige" and as "a monument to American money."[90]

South Florida was, as Mizner helps to illuminate, prominently depicted to be a capitalist utopia where the rich could get richer and the working class, if they were just smart enough to play their cards right, could transcend to a higher social class. Miami was, in other words, depicted the be the Miami Dream – the bigger and better consumerist version of the American Dream.

By the time former Populist presidential candidate William Jennings Bryan took up residence on the Gold Coast in 1913, Southeast Florida had long been marketed nationwide as the "playground of the elite" and "winter capital of

---

[89] Donald W. Curl, *Mizner's Florida*, (Cambridge, MA: MIT Press, 1984), pp. 14.

[90] *Palm Beach Post*, September 5, 1925.

American high society."[91] But by the mid-1920s, tens of thousands of middle-class and working-class folks anxious for action and access to a higher class of consumerism had arrived in Miami in search of the Miami Dream, social mobility via mass consumption (rather than hard work and austerity). Most of those who made the rush to Miami by the 1920s were a veritable cross-section of American life: the butcher, baker, as well as bankers and speculators from big cities, "and also from Main Street, and from the country behind Main Street" they came, the *World's Work* reported. The greater part of them, the leftist newspaper noted, came to Miami deliberately "to buy;" while others came for winter months on a vacation but had "caught the fever and become property owners." The bulk of the purchasers were, the *World's Work* lamented, "hardworking, middle-class, small town folks."[92]

These "folks" were lured, in part, by ads that depicted Miami to be a capitalist utopia. During and after World War I, the City Council increasingly used the latest in communication technologies such as billboards, brochures, films, gramophone, and postcards to market Miami to a wider cross-section of Americans. Boosters used communication technology to showcase Miami both as a sensual city of romance as well as a suburban oasis where both profits and

---

[91] See Larry R. Youngs, "The Sporting Set Winters in Florida: Fertile Ground for the Leisure Revolution, 1870-1930," *The Florida Historical Quarterly*, Vol. 84, No. 1, Special H-Florida Issue: Florida History from Transnational Perspectives (summer, 2005), pp. 57–78.

[92] Reginald T. Townsend, "Gold Rush to Florida," *World's Work* 50 June 1925, 179.

beautiful women seemed synonymous to South Florida. *Miami* (1924), a talkie produced by the City Council, regaled viewers with tales of "pleasure-mad rich" Florida, where profit could be easily plucked like low-hanging citrus.[93] Film and newsreels also informed Americans that Miami was not far from the northeast by car, rail, and regular steamship line. Ads also synergistically informed consumers of Miami's growing list of urban amenities and exploitable opportunities. The ads did the trick. South Florida's population boomed all through the 1920s.

Mary Louise Roberts wrote that by the twentieth century, advertisers in places like New York, Chicago, London, and Paris began to change the meaning and purpose of commodities via advertising. Whereas products were previously the source of enjoyment, by the twentieth century, they, as Thornstein Veblen likewise noted, were increasingly subordinate to the quest for social status. Miami was, however, conversely marketed as a source of enjoyment, magical transcendence, and, concomitantly, a conspicuous designator of social status.[94] For example, numerous "success stories" (some true, most fabricated) of persons who had become wealthy overnight through South Florida real estate

---

[93] "How *Miami*, the Movie, is the Advertising City, World," *Miami Herald*, May 18,1924, 12A; see also Kenneth Roberts, *Sun Hunting* (Indianapolis, 1922), 5, 139, 167, and 186; and also Kenneth Roberts, *Florida Loafing* (Indianapolis, 1924); and also Shelton S. Matlack, "Watch for Florida in the Movies," *Suniland* 2, April 1925, 22–25.

[94] Mary Louise Roberts, "Gender, Consumption, and Commodity Culture," The American Historical Review, Vol. 103, No. 3 (Jun., 1998), pp. 817–844. See also Thorstein Veblen, whose Theory of the Leisure Class (1899).

speculation were often disseminated throughout the country in magazines designed for both men and women – such as *McClure's, Outlook,* and *Field and Stream*, as well as trade publications such as the *Wall Street Journal*. Even *Time Magazine* advertised Coral Gables with a booklet titled "2% to 4% Extra (on money invested within the year)." The ad boasts of a buyer gaining $7,208 in principal and an increase in income of $1,077 and promises "no risk."[95]

The value of homeownership and automobiles had long been self-evident by the 1920s.[96] Creditors, however, had to convince consumers that going into debt was a wise investment and thus in their best interest. Packaging debt as sound securities such as a family home helped transform the idea of debt from socially unacceptable to a potential avenue of social mobility. Long before the 1929 stock market crash that plunged the industrialized world into economic depression, lenders with access to mass marketing religiously proliferated the notion across the social spectrum that everyone's piece of the economic pie could expand exponentially by investing in South Florida land.

By the 1920s, otherwise reputable and widely respected publications

---

[95] *Time*, December 14, 1925, 32; and *Miami Herald*, November 30, 1925.

[96] "Only at home," John Tosh argues of Englishmen in the nineteenth century, "could a man be truly and authentically himself." Tosh defines the cult of domesticity as distinct from sheer domestic life and as a nineteenth-century invention, an affective ideal "grounded above all in a sense of alienation from the social and moral consequences of industrialism" See Tosh, *A Man's Place: Masculinity and the Middle-Class Home in Victorian England* (New Haven, CT and London: Yale University Press, 1999), 33 and 178.

including *The New York Times* and *The Saturday Evening Post* were heavily involved, if not also invested, in imbuing "value" in South Florida land, much of which was submerged under putrid swamp water. Miami's image was, however, consistently glamorized in ads in northern newspapers and magazines as *the* city to match 1920s excess. Utopian depictions of Miami often made it seem as though easy profit waited for the taking, and Florida — especially South Florida — was a "latter day gold rush."[97] In February 1925, for example, before the structural deficiencies of the boom had become too terribly glaring, J.B. Hecht, the President of the Mortgage Security Corporation of America, a man who had spent ten days on the Gold Coast and had made a "thorough" study of loan conditions, was quoted by *The Miami Herald*, as saying that, although he had come prejudiced against Miami due to wild tales of exorbitant land prices, he returned to Norfolk, Virginia, "satisfied that Florida's rapid expansion was "not of a boom character, but . . . based upon sound fundamentals." Felix Isman, writing for *The Saturday Evening Post*, likewise wrote that Miami's boom was not an ordinary one; it was unlike an oil or gold discovery; Florida had none of the privations of the Klondike or "Pike's Peak or Bust," he wrote. Florida, which had lagged behind in national development well into the twentieth century, was, Isman deduced, finally "coming into its own."[98] Financier Charles E. Forbes was

---

[97] Eun Choi Kyou, "Florida Business Cycles, 1920–1960," (Ph.D. dissertation, University of Florida, 1964), 117.

[98] See Frank B. Sessa, "Miami on the Eve of the Boom: 1925" *Tequesta*, No. XI, 1951.

also quoted in a *Miami Herald* article saying of the boom in Miami, "just so long as people continue to read ads and are influenced by them to act, Florida will prosper." He editorialized that Miami's meteoric rise would continue so long as Florida had the climate and resources, and people had money to invest. "No one," he wrote, "asks when the boom in New York is going to break simply because several thousand people are engaged in nothing else than speculation."[99] A booster publication from April of 1925 seconded the notion by declaring that Miami was "not having a boom like the West where professional speculators made paper towns out of nothing, disposed of lots and went their way to pastures green."[100]

Reports of marked gains in the city's financial and municipal institutions, services, and amenities also routinely found their way into *The New York Times, Wall Street Journal,* as well as *The Commercial and Financial Chronicle.* News reports and ads seemed to synergistically convince scores of consumers that Miami was a utopian site of social mobility. Thousands of speculators had thus become the unlucky owners of lots that were still under water due to the "value" concocted by utopian mass marketing of Miami as an avenue of social mobility that

---

[99] Frank B. Sessa, "Anti-Florida Propaganda and Counter Measures during the 1920's," *Tequesta*, pp. 41–51; 43.

[100] Ballinger, *Miami Millions,* 41.

promised "no risk."[101]

October 26, 1926 — a month after a hurricane with 125-mile-per hour winds rocked several ramshackle construction projects in Miami — Florida Governor John W. Martin met with business and political leaders and editors from the *Literary Digest* and *World's Work* and a number of newspapers at the "Truth About Florida" public relations event at Coleman du Pont's Waldorf Astoria Hotel in midtown Manhattan. The gathering was also attended by scores of investors in Florida land schemes such as Barron Collier, S. Davies Warfield, and du Pont himself, who had an interest in Mizner's Boca Raton land scheme. During the Waldorf event, speakers referred to "degrading" stories published about the Gold Coast in various newspapers throughout the nation "as propaganda against Florida." Walter W. Rose, President of the Florida Association of Real Estate Boards, for instance, said the negative publicity against Florida "must be combated, for it attacked unfairly the state's vast resources like agriculture, phosphates, and fruit." Duke A. de Richelieu, who had an interest in Fort Lauderdale, just north of Miami, referred to negative press directed against South Florida speculation as "an attack upon mobile capital," and it, therefore, "endeavored to strike at the very foundations of modern business organization."[102] Various speakers stated that the real estate activity in Florida

---

[101] Bruce Bliven, "Where Ev'ry Prospect Pleases," *New Republic*, 38 (March 26, 1924), 117, and Lyman Delano, "Florida's Transportation Problems," *Independent* 116 (January 23, 1926) 104.

[102] Sessa, "Anti-Florida Propaganda and Counter Measures during the 1920's."

did not constitute a boom, per se, but rather "the great increase in values only represented real worth" so long as people believed it did.

The cadre of capitalists assembled at the Waldorf Astoria who held economic interest in fueling South Florida speculation especially combated the negative press in the months after the meeting. They defended Miami as if the city were capitalism itself. *The Atlanta Constitution*, for instance, published an article that praised the Miami City Commission's role in keeping the city open for business after the hurricane. "The complete rehabilitation of Miami following the terrible hurricane damages of a few months ago," the article stated, "stands out in American history as a marvelous example of community spirit, and as an even more marvelous example of efficiency in municipal government." The utopian article further states, "The government of Miami is held as a great business enterprise, requiring the application of the same sound, sane, time-tested economic principles that make private businesses a success… Miami's freedom of political discord, her marvelous record for advancement, her phenomenal recovery from storm and hectic flush of speculative inflation, prove beyond even the shadow of a doubt the efficiency of such a system."[103] Ads published in February of 1927 by the Miami Real Estate and Building Company

---

[103] *The Atlanta Constitution*, "How Miami Did It," Jan 12, 1927, 4. Miami's commission form of government coincided with the real estate boom. The commission was voted into effect May 1921. See also *The Christian Science Monitor,* June 1, 8. Women, who cast 1300 votes, were essential to passage.

likewise claimed that the city's recent construction activity "surpasse[d] any similar growth the world has ever known" and noted that "students of economics and sound businessmen base the stability of any real estate activity on the amount of building activity which accompanies the land boom." The office buildings, hotels, apartments, and causeways already erected in Miami should, another ad stated, "firmly convince you that the city of Miami is building its golden future on a lasting foundation of cement and steel" and for "permanence."[104] An ad for Miami Shores likewise rhetorically queried consumers: "do you suppose that such institutions as J.P. Morgan & Company would offer such securities if Florida did not warrant their sale? Then why bother asking questions as to the stability of Florida and the South?" *The Wall Street Journal* likewise declared in February 1927, "Florida is now central in American development and there is no section of it more in the public eye than Miami and its suburbs." The article, of course, highlighted Miami as a "sound investment."[105]

But in the end, these ads proved erroneous for many investors. The amount of individual and corporate financial ruin associated with the 1920s land boom/bust – which was a generation in the making, thanks in part to utopian ads of Miami – was incalculable. Unfounded confidence in notions of continual

---

[104] *New York Times*, November 11 and 18, 1925.

[105] *The Wall Street Journal*, "Reports Reveal Miami's Growth," February 12, 1927.

profits in South Florida commercial and residential real estate prices prompted too rapid an expansion of debt through the 1910s and 1920s. Bonds sold by Florida's Drainage District in the interest of transforming the South Florida frontier into real estate values helped inflate the general bond market throughout the U.S. in the decades prior to the 1930s. The speculative frenzy in South Florida real estate during the 1920s led many municipalities on the peninsula to institute costly internal improvement programs financed by the sale of bonds. The onset of the bust, and the consequent loss of anticipated revenue owing to the non-payment of taxes, left some South Florida communities with long-term debts that caused the level of property taxes to spike drastically, and placed severe limitations on cities' abilities to provide anything but the most basic public services.[106] And by the 1929 stock market implosion, Drainage District bonds had suffered the same steep decline as other bonds throughout the nation. On January 1, 1931, the Drainage District finally defaulted and spiraled into bankruptcy. Florida's taxpayers, many of whom were lured to the region by utopian advertisements that promised traditional racial and gender norms and social mobility, were forced to bail out the bonded indebtedness created by the real estate barons, bankers, ad men and publications most responsible for

---

[106] Paul S. George, "Brokers, Binders, and Builders: Greater Miami's Boom of the Mid-1920s," *The Florida Historical Quarterly*, Vol. 65, No. 1 (Jul., 1986), pp. 27-51, 50.

marketing Miami as a natural oasis and escape from the filth, crime, and grime of so many other industrialized cities in the early decades of the twentieth century.[107]

---

[107] Lemar Stephan, "Historico-Economic Aspects of Drainage in the Florida Everglades," *Southern Economic Journal*, Vol. 10, No. 3 (Jan., 1944), pp. 197-211), 209.

This 1912 brochure, which includes marketing of Miami, depicts East Florida as a site of idle luxury and retreat for society's elites. These images of urbane white affluence are in stark contrast to images depicting Seminole Indians and black Floridians as rural yokels (see chapter three of this study). "The Florida East Coast Railway and Its Magnificent Hotels," Florida East Coast Railway, Saint Augustine, Florida, 1912, page 1. University of Miami Library, Special Collections, ASC9999 F316 F6945 1912.

Florida was often depicted to be the scene of a fairy tale where wishes were waiting to come true for consumers eager to transcend the harsh realities of the hard labor and cold winters synonymous with northern industrialization. "Florida East Coast: The Winter Vacation Land," Florida East Coast Railway, Saint Augustine, Florida, 1918. University of Miami Library, Special Collections, ASC9999 F309.3.F54 1918.

This 1920s brochure for Miami Beach accentuates the Gatsby-like white aristocrat high culture image civic elites sought to define the city according to. It also evokes the moonlight and magnolia iconography that was so often used to market New South cities in the early decades of the twentieth century. What is also interesting is the lovers' gaze not looking inward across the continent, but out towards the Atlantic Ocean, as if to indicate that the U.S. was, by the 1920s, a global empire. "Miami Beach: America's Playground," (Miami Beach Chamber of Commerce, early 1920s); Smathers Library Ephemera Collection, University of Florida, folder 37 number 1066.

The cover of this 1923 brochure marketing Miami Beach blends the objectification of the "New Woman" motif with aristocracy, particularly Polo – the "sport of kings." It is also interesting to note the American flag waiving in the background, thereby conflating capitalism, affluent leisure, and nationalism in South Florida's commoditized form. "Miami Beach, Florida," St. Augustine, Florida Record Co.,1923, page 1. University of Miami Library, Special Collections, ASC9999 F319.M62. M48 1923.

The oft-depicted Miami as a consumerist utopia of affluent leisure is in stark contrast to Fordist depictions of Detroit and Taylorist depictions of Cleveland, New York City, Chicago, and European cities during the same time period. "Miami, Florida, By the Sea," City of Miami Publicity Department, 1928, page 1. University of Miami Library, Special Collections, ASC9999 F319.M6 M624 1928.

Ads such as this conspicuously promise entry into a higher social class via land speculation in South Florida. *McClure's Magazine*, Volume 54, number 7, September 1922, S.S. McClure publishing, 120.

Mexico, and Central and South America large quantities, bringing the supply to $501,640,000. After the discovery of gold in California and Australia, in 1849-51, there was a big jump in the world supply, which by 1890 was estimated at $4,806,866,000. Later discoveries in various places, including the Klondyke, Nevada, and the Transvaal, brought the estimated world supply to sixteen billion dollars by 1914, some of which was used in the arts and industry, some in bullion and coin by nations. The double standard of gold and silver had long prevailed, in a haphazard manner, and it was only in 1816, when there was enough gold to meet commercial uses, that England adopted the single or gold standard, followed by Germany in 1871, the United States in 1873, and France in 1876.

The largest producers of gold until 1914 were the United States with 3,913, Australia with 3,261, and Africa with 3,263 billion dollars.

The United States, which had started the mint coinage of gold in 1791, had coined, by 1911, $3,271,514,410. Much of this gold had been sold, however, in the course of trade or to pay balances due Europe. At the beginning of the world war the United States' basic gold metallic stock was roughly 1,866 million dollars, that of Great Britain 1,600, of France 1,200, Russia 1,200 and Germany 1,000. At least another billion was held in Austria and Italy.

If ever there was an age of gold, it was in the period that ended in 1914. There was not only plenty of gold to regulate international commerce, but also enough to be used as coined money for internal circulation in the richer countries. Gold came to be accepted as a basic fact of every day life like bread. And man's life went on peacefully. He was occupied with moral problems no more disturbing than the prevention of cruelty to animals. He had enough food, clothes, enough gold. Paper money was the equivalent of gold in most countries. The people of Switzerland and Austria preferred paper money to gold coin. In England, France, and Germany, gold coin circulated as freely as silver in the United States, where we find gold too heavy, too easy to lose. Among these three na-

(Continued on page 474)

This ad promises an astounding $2,000 for a .65-cent investment in South Florida real estate. *McClure's Magazine* (1893 to 1926), Volume 1, Issue 3, July 1925, 471.

should be paid each year on a mathematical basis which will yield a sum sufficient to carry on the expense of the business and allow for sums due on the maturity of policies. The competition is keen and rates are kept down to substantially an irreducible minimum. Able management and aggressive sales organizations have, as a rule, enabled the stock life insurance companies to compete successfully with the mutual companies and also as a rule there has been a somewhat more rapid gain in growth of stock companies than in mutuals, measured by insurance underwritten. All of which has favored a gradual increment to the value of life insurance company stocks.

That this has been remarkable in instances can be indicated by a few examples. Not long ago an authority on insurance stocks estimated that if an investor had subscribed at par $100 a share to one share of stock at the Aetna Life Insurance Company in 1850 and assuming that he had retained all stocks dividends and subscribed to all increases in capital stock, he would now have 66 shares of stock, at a total cost of $2933. At present market prices these holdings would now be worth $78,658 and the annual dividends thereon, at the present rate of $12 a share annually, would be $792 a year. Of course this is an extreme and probably theoretical case. Nevertheless the purchaser of the stock in 1914 who took advantage of the rights accruing over the past eleven years would have received by the first of this year an average annual return in cash dividends and market appreciation of about 31 per cent. In the same period an investment in the Travelers Insurance Company would have returned an average of 22 per cent in cash dividends and market appreciation.

### Fire Insurance Stocks

Fire insurance stocks, as investments, involve a somewhat different principle. Life insurance companies invest their funds in bonds. Bonds are payable in dollars and policies are payable in dollars. It is of no concern to the life insurance company whether the purchasing power of the dollar rises or falls. An inflation such as occurred in the German mark might conceivably efface all value to the life company's investments and reserves, but it would also efface all liability for policies

This ad for Florida land conspicuously packages land speculation as a "sound security." *Forum* (1886 to 1930) Volume LXXIV, number 1, July 1925, 156.

# Coda

Miami was in some ways as much a "harbinger of modernity" as the Coney Island depicted in John Kasson's *Amusing the Million*.[108] Like Kasson's depiction of Coney Island, Miami acted as both a mechanism of social release and control, which ultimately protected the existing social order, and which evolved from planter paternalism and the factory system into mass consumerism and urbanization. The late-nineteenth-century values generally associated with an agrarian producing society, such as thrift, hard work, punctuality, and delayed gratification, gradually gave way to a new set of values more appropriate to an all-consuming, commercialized, urban-industrial modern society. This new set of values was the lifeblood of both thrill parks, such as Coney Island, as well as resort cities such as Atlantic City, Las Vegas, and Miami.

Miami's growth and development was also, in some ways, comparable to "instant cities" such as San Francisco and Denver, which lured fortune seekers to the American West in the nineteenth century. What made twentieth-century South Florida's growth and development a brand apart from all these places was, however, the notion that its greatest assets – unlike the mineral and precious metal booms out west or the overt gambling that lured folks to Las Vegas and

---

[108] John F. Kasson, *Amusing the Million: Coney Island at the Turn of the Century*, (New York: Hill & Wang, 1978) 8. Titles also related to *Marketing Miami* include: Charles E. Funnell's, *By the Beautiful Sea: The Rise and High Times of That Great American Resort, Atlantic City*; Barbara Berglund's, *Making San Francisco American: Cultural Frontiers in the Urban West, 1846–1906*; and Angela M. Blake's, *How New York Became American, 1890–1924*.

Atlantic City – were the tropical weather and cheap land, both of which were depicted as antidotes to the pollution, tenement housing, crime, and social despair and decay often associated with industrialized cities in Europe and the United States. Miami's image, which promised consumers a suburban oasis, imperial nationalism, traditional racial and gender mores, and quick and easy social mobility, was ultimately designed to assuage anxiety associated with urban-industrial society in order to promote economic growth, all while retaining the existing social order that had long shaped American society.

Marketing of Miami in the early decades of the twentieth century helps to illuminate that "modern" race relations equated to a white supremacy that was as central to the urbanization of the New South, including Miami, as it was to the Old South's rural plantocracy. And, although marketing of Miami in the early decades of the twentieth century at times seemed to celebrate the dawn of the "New Woman," it simultaneously celebrated Victorian gender norms, especially heteronormative family values. Also, while Miami was being marketed as an epicenter of social mobility, the get-rich-quick ethos associated with the "Magic City" ultimately ended in countless calamites for nearly all but the most affluent real estate barons invested in sundry land schemes.

In short, beneath the air of leisure and liberation imbued in Miami's commoditized form, the celebration of consumer capitalism embedded in the "Magic City's" image was profoundly conformist and conservative and, ultimately, served the interests of the existing social order. In that sense, the American brand of modernity rooted in mass consumption is, perhaps above all else, best understood as a marketing construct shilling old wine in "new and improved" bottles, thus underscoring the idea that one of the primary mechanisms that make the endless accumulation of capital possible is the commodification of everything, including nationalism, race, sex, gender, class, and entire cities such as Miami, New York, Paris, and London; metropolises where rents and public services had, by the turn of the twenty-first century, gotten so astronomical that few members of the working class could even afford to live in them.